Literary Gems

Lydia Bongcaron Wade

authorHOUSE®

AuthorHouse™
1663 Liberty Drive
Bloomington, IN 47403
www.authorhouse.com
Phone: 1 (800) 839-8640

Published by AuthorHouse 06/23/2016

ISBN: 978-1-5246-1351-8 (sc)
ISBN: 978-1-5246-1350-1 (e)

Print information available on the last page.

Any people depicted in stock imagery provided by Thinkstock are models,
and such images are being used for illustrative purposes only.
Certain stock imagery © Thinkstock.

This book is printed on acid-free paper.

Because of the dynamic nature of the Internet, any web addresses or links contained in
this book may have changed since publication and may no longer be valid. The views
expressed in this work are solely those of the author and do not necessarily reflect the
views of the publisher, and the publisher hereby disclaims any responsibility for them.

Dedicated to Those Who
Love to Read

This is a compilation of different types of literature:
jokes, short stories, essays, dialogues, poetry and words
of wisdom.

Lydia Bongcaron Wade

PART 1

Humor (Original) Let's Laugh!

Father and Son

A father and his 8 eight year old son were walking their dog, Celeste on a spring morning. "Father," the son asked. Why are you not picking up Celeste's waste?" "The father smiled and said, "Our new neighbors need them to fertilize their vegetable garden."

The Mother's Song

"Mother, why are you crying?" The mother wiped away her tears and said to her four year old son," I have sung four songs already but your little brother refuses to sleep." "He is listening to your song. See? Perhaps he wants to be a singer one day."

A Sad Story

Marian just lost her husband to cancer. A friend whispered to her at the wake." I know you are grieving, but Leon is waiting for you at the Village Restaurant for your lunch date."

The New Army Recruit

On Mark Holt's first day with his platoon, while they were marching through a marsh land, the sergeant suddenly stopped and shouted to his men. Halt! "Aye, Aye sir!" Mark Holt bolted forward with a salute.

False Tears

Rosalind took a big serving of Nigerian stew and started eating. Her tears were falling while eating the spicy but delicious stew. "Why are you crying, dear? Her Nigerian boyfriend Matthew's mother remarked. "I just remembered my mother. She is a terrific cook like you."

The Inheritance

An old, ailing grandpa lay dying. His 16 year old grandson came and held his hand. "Grandpa, I don't want you to die," Joseph wept. Don't cry, my favorite grandson. When I die you will get your inheritance, a hefty sum." "True, grandpa? Then, please go soon. I want to buy my own car!" Joseph declared happily.

Great Lover

Man to his girlfriend: "Louise, call Martha. I want her to pick me up tonight." "Who is Martha? My third girlfriend." Brute!" Louise screamed at him.

A Grandson's Love

"Armand, Do you love me?" Of course, grandpa. Very much! "Hold my hand." "My lovable grandson, do you love me? Grandpa asked again. "Surely, grandpa." Armand said solemnly, holding his grandpa's hand. "My dear boy, do you love me?" "Because you keep on repeating your question, I do not love you any longer." Armand declared indignantly.

Mother and Daughter

A mother took her 16-year old daughter aside and said," Amy, I do not want you to get married until you are above 20. "But mother, I am already married to Richard!"

Fishing in the River

"Boys, see the sign there? You have to throw back your catch into the lake." One of Joe's sons left and came back later. "Father, look over there. There is a new sign, "Throw your catch into your basket."

Mom's Recipe

Lilibeth, six years old, went to her mother in the kitchen with a written recipe and said," Mom, would you cook this meal for me?" The mother looked and replied, "Why, this recipe seems really good. Where did you get it?" From your collection, where else?"

Bill and Lenny

Bill and Lenny hitched a ride to the park with their friend's older brother, Mario. "Could you please stop at the gas station?" "I am in a rush. I can't stop now." "But Mario, the boys spoke at the same time. "Your tank is empty!"

The Lonely Traveler

Marsha, an old maid loved to travel. She was relaxing on St. Lucie's pristine beach one morning when a handsome man sat beside her. "Enjoying the beach? The man asked. "Oh, Lucio! Come closer. I really missed you!" Surprised, the man stood up and said, "Why, lady, I never saw you before in my life!"

A Hearty Confession

As Johnny knelt in the Confessional waiting for the priest to turn to him, he did not know what to say. He could not think of any sin to confess. When the priest was ready for him, Johnny said in a hushed voice, "Father Stephen, I have to confess honestly. I saw you last night at the theater with a young, beautiful woman."

Beautiful Lenora

Ralph and his new girlfriend, Lenora were sitting on the veranda, gazing at the full moon. "Sweetheart, I am very happy to be your boyfriend. You are so beautiful!" Lenora stood up and said, sounding annoyed. "My other boyfriends say that I am not only beautiful but fun and smart!"

Her Little Pony

"Madeline, your father and I have a surprise for you." The mother told her daughter on her 5ᵗʰ birthday. When the girl saw the pony, she jumped with joy. Just then, one of two uniformed men came and said. "We have your husband in custody ma'am, for stealing that pony."

Enchanted Bridge?

Two boys were about to cross a bridge one evening when a tall man confronted them. "Run, Mario, run!" Jessie screamed. But Mario stood his ground. He held Jessie's arm and said. "Don't get scared, Jessie. That's only my older brother. He died the other day."

Double Divorce

"The wife confronted her husband at the door. "You unfaithful brute! I saw you with Susie. I want a divorce! "The husband replied calmly. "I would have said the same thing to you, you know. Susie said that her husband dated you twice last month."

To Obey or Not?

Charlotte emphasized "obedience" to her children. One morning, her youngest son, Phillip's teacher called her. "Mrs. Wolbrook, your son is at the Juvenile Detention Center. He reportedly stole garden tools from his classmate's yard."

When Charlotte visited her son, Phillip said tearfully. "Father asked me to do it. He wants to start gardening this week."

Wedding Blues

Before "I do" was said at Josh's and Meredith's wedding, Meredith excused herself.

Horrified, her groom, Josh asked. "Where are you going, darling?" "I have to go to the train station. Gerard and I are going to elope."

His Duty

Alphonse was granted two weeks furlough from his tour in Afghanistan. "What are you going to do during your leave, buddy?" His bunker mate, Manny asked. "Sh! Sh! Don't tell anyone. I would like to join my uncle who is with Isis in the mountains of Syria."

What a Day!

Selma, 12 and her sister Joyce, 14 were arguing hard. ""You took my Ipad!" "No! I did not!" Back and forth they screamed at each other. The mother had an idea. "Marco," she called her husband. "Help me with your daughters." "I have an urgent report to write," retorted Marco. Can't you spare a second to make them stop?" "I told you I am busy!" The couple argued until it became a shouting match. Selma and Joyce stopped their fighting.

To Make Her Happy

A doting sister asked her younger sister who was suffering with Leukemia. "Sweetie, ask me anything, anything at all and I shall give it to you."" Are you sure?" The sick child asked wearily. Take my pains away, please."

Flowers for Mom

Every morning, Marianne surprised her mother with a bunch of fresh flowers. One day, when all the rooms were filled with vases full of flowers, the mother asked. "Marianne, where did you get the money to pay for all the flowers?" "I got it from your piggy bank."

When Hope was Gone

Rey was a desperate man. He lost his wife last year, then his house was taken by the IRS because he has failed to pay taxes for three consecutive years. His three children in High School quit because they could not pay even for school supplies.

He took his children to the edge of the cliff and said to them. "Whoever jumps over with me will get a just reward." "What reward, father?" The oldest son asked. "A seat beside me in heaven."

The Blind Professor

"Listen, everyone," his opening words to a class of 15 unruly students. I can't see you or what you are doing, and hear you, but mind, I would always know what you are up to. A naughty student came forward and stood behind the professor's back. "You are old, useless and smelling." With this remark, the student hit him and spat on him.

The security detail whisked the student away after the professor fingered him. He was the Dean of the College disguised as a blind professor.

A Broken Promise

Before he left to join the U.S. Navy, Herman made a promise to his wife. "Be patient, my love. I shall be back before you know it. On my first leave in eight months, we shall go together to a place you always dreamed of going, Bermuda.

Eight long weeks passed and the wife was filled with joyful anticipation for the husband's return. He never did. Later, she learned that her beloved had eloped with his sergeant's wife to Bermuda.

Leonora's Return

Leonora has been gone for two years. Her old mother asked anxiously, "My child, where have you been?" I went away to get out of this house and from you." So, why did you return?" "I thought you were dead. I wanted to claim my inheritance."

Jose's Promise

"My darling, I love you so much I could cry. Let us get married now." "Oh, no. I do not want a crying baby of a husband."

The Hurricane

A father gathered all his family in their basement shelter to escape the strong hurricane. He noticed that his oldest son was missing. "Where is Arnie?" His wife answered, "He is out there, trying to stop the hurricane."

Hateful

"I hate you, Ray. You are always nowhere whenever I need you." "What do you need me for? Isn't Ed enough for you?"

Ann's Gift

"Come here, Ann," her father called her only daughter. I have a most precious gift for you." "What is it, father?" Ann opened the box anxiously. Inside were ashes of her dear deceased mother. "I'd like you to keep the box with you so that she would be able to watch you when I am away."

Painful Gratitude

'I am greatly indebted to you, my dear friend," Simon said to his friend, Danny. Someone close to you has been really taking care of me. Yeah? Who is the person? Your caring wife, Louise."

No Smarter than the Other

Danilo and Johan are inseparable friends. Both are wise and smart. One day, they came upon a deep lake.

"Let's see who between us is the smarter. Johan asked. Tell me, what is the name of this lake and who named it? "That's easy. The name is Danilo, and the one who named it is Johan." Wrong. The name is Johan, and Danilo, me, gave it its name."

Incredible Nimo

Nimo is very tall, big and strong for his age of 12. His friends taunted him one day. "Nimo, if you can lift me and put me on your shoulder, we shall give you a big prize. "If I lift you three all at once, will you triple the prize?" Nimo asked. As Nimo prepared to lift the boys, they all ran away.

PART II

Original Short Stories and Essays (Fiction and Non-Fiction)

My Thoughts About God

God is in my thoughts and in my heart every day. There isn't a single time that I don't invoke Him in my daily life, through prayers and meditation. It is not just an expression or a fleeting thought that I say, I trust in His mercy completely, His bountiful graces, blessings and His forgiveness, which He readily gives to anyone, to everyone who asks for them. He is woven in every fiber of my being, intermingled with His poor creation, "my lowly self."

He is the beginning, the end of everyone's life and everything in this earth. Anyone who does not believe Him as our Supreme Creator and Savior is lost, like a grain of sand that crumbles and disappears amid the onslaught of the waves lapping on the shore of eternity.

There were countless circumstances in my life when I have felt and enjoyed God's unfailing grace and mercy. Praise Him! My life has been full of trials, from the simplest and the least important to the most significant. Often, in my weakness, I complain too. Yet He always prevails. He beckons and prods me to continue to carry my crosses, as He carried His cross on Mt. Calvary. I should be glad to have a small share of His sufferings.

Unbelievable, impossible situations in my life could only be explained as Divine Interventions. I have related many of my misfortunes, mostly happening in a far country in Africa verbally and in writing. My books touch on some of those circumstances.

It was God's plan to take me to a backward, poor country where dangers were lurking everywhere. Crossing an old bridge one day after Teaching Practice supervision of college students assigned in a tiny village, my car nearly fell into a dry, stony river. Only a couple of inches more and I would have hurtled into the stony grave below. With no alternative route, I drove between two burning hills and felt the scorching heat on both sides of me, but I came out unscathed. Driving into kilometers of wilderness inhabited by cannibals and hostile natives were feats that make me shiver now just remembering them. I never encountered any of them and I never once had a flat tire.

I faced imminent danger from insect and poisonous snake bites, often endured malaria in spite of preventive medications. Two of my colleagues died of the dreaded Ebola virus. Life day by day was a constant threat to survival, an uncertainty, a gloomy, debilitating feeling. Loneliness living alone in the midst of the jungle was killing too. I did not know where I got the courage to go on, but I continued to pray.

Transferred to the southwest of the country, which I believed was more civilized than the north east, I was confronted by a furious mob with hatchets and knives one afternoon when I wandered into their religious rituals by mistake. A kind gentleman intervened. My car fell into a deep cliff, but miraculously, I came out with just bruises.

I had encountered many other inexplicable, life-threatening incidents in my life before, which seemed hard to believe, but true. As they continued to happen, I hang on, supported by fervent prayers and an unwavering faith in the power and mercy of the One and True God.

After the Rain

Wisdom for us all to know;
Peace greater after pain,
God's covenant the rainbow-
Comes only after the rain!
By Le Rochefaucauld

The receptionist at the Food Stamps Office in Jamaica, Queens, New York, handed Mercedes a number and said. "Wait for your number to be called. Get ready with your papers." The line at the reception area was long, extending to the entrance of the Human Resources Building on 5th St. this early October morning.

As she waited for her number to be called, Mercedes sat down on the only vacant chair in the waiting area and examined her papers for EVR) Eligibility Verification Review.) Her Food Stamps benefits had expired. She failed to show up for her previous interview because she was ill. She also did not have money to fill in her Metro card for the subway ride. Her neighbor at the Section 8

Housing in Woodside lent her $5.00 for her ride today, to be repaid with groceries when she got back her benefits.

It had been a tough year for Mercedes, tougher than the two previous years since she lost her job as secretary at a State-funded program in Richmond Hill, Queens. Many such programs in New York had been closed due to lack of funding. Her husband died a year ago of pneumonia. He left her nothing, not even Social Security benefits because he did not work long enough to qualify for the Federal program. She did not qualify for it either. Her only option was to apply for Public Assistance benefits.

Her social worker's intervention saved her from being thrown into the streets when she could not pay her rent by giving her a room to stay while waiting for her subsidized apartment. Her oldest son got into drugs and was in and out of Rehab. The second son, Julio died in a car accident six months ago. Lizzie, her third child married an alcoholic. He was abusive and cruel. Lizzie moved to Texas with her young son. She seldom called her and when she did, it was only to ask for help. Mercedes' youngest daughter took off to seek employment in a place she did not know. She never called or wrote to her.

Mercedes broke down when the Entitlement Specialist told her that she lacked some required documentation. "I can only give you emergency grant for two weeks. Come back next week with the rest of the papers."

The phone was ringing when she got home. "Mother, we are moving back home. We have been evicted. And, (sob) your grandson has been diagnosed with Leukemia." Mercedes wept. "Is there no let up from the storms in my life?" An urgent knocking on her front door jolted her. "Mama, Are you in there?" It was a voice she did not hear in a long time. She almost passed out when she opened the door.

"Mama, don't you recognize me?" "Luz? Is it really you? Mercedes returned her daughter's embrace. She could hardly believe her eyes. She had not seen her in five years. "You look so fabulous! So beautiful!" She surveyed Luz dressed in expensive clothes and glittering jewelry. "You look unbelievably rich! How would I recognize you?" "Mother, you look so thin. I almost did not recognize you myself."

The story Luz told her mother was like a fairy tale. Her employer in Italy, a very wealthy man, married her. Guiseppe died of a heart attack a few months back. He left her several holdings, a villa in Nice, France, vacation homes in Barcelona and ranch estates in Madrid. He had a large deposit in a Swiss bank. It was an awesome, incredible fortune.

Luz bought her mother a mansion along the Hudson river in Upstate, New York. Mercedes opted to remain in America than live in Europe. Luz' next priorities were her siblings and her ailing nephew.

The skies cleared up early in the morning after a steady downpour last night. "What a divine morning!" Mercedes exclaimed from her balcony overlooking the awesome Hudson Valley with the mighty Hudson River shimmering in the early morning glow as it flowed steadily along. A rainbow arched behind the mesmerizing fall foliage along the New Jersey Shore. She heaved a long, happy sigh and proclaimed, "My rainbow!"

Blindness, A Curse

My maternal grandma became blind at the age of 55, a diabetic complication. Eye surgeries during that period were expensive and rare, and the eye doctor was half a day away, so Grandma Lina did not want to be bothered even for an examination. She was also afraid going to the doctor, let alone, going under the knife. She opted to bear her infirmity and accepted it quite gallantly. She remained alone in their ancestral home long after my grandpa died of pneumonia. Life expectancy was then shorter than now. Those who lived past fifty were considered lucky.

I was eleven years old and in grade school when I was assigned to help grandma after school hours. My only brother and four sisters, all in high school, stayed in boarding homes next town and came home only during Sundays. Although they also helped whenever they could, I bore most of the burden helping grandma along with my two cousins. Keeping grandma company especially during nights, do housework and running errands kept us busy.

Grandma Lina was a very independent old woman. She would insist moving about by herself without help. One day, she nearly fell over the wooden bridge connecting the house to the toilet. My cousin barely caught her. Another day, she wanted to bathe in the river instead of inside the house. She insisted on going alone, reminding us that she had memorized the path to the river having lived there all her married life. Besides, the river was only a short distance away.

To get to the river, she had to follow a path across a rice field. There were men harvesting rice in the field, so we allowed her to go alone. We also kept an eye on her as we played jumping rope. We heard her cry as she stumbled into the rice paddy with waist deep, murky water. A worker saw her struggling in the water and rescued her before we got to her. We were punished when my aunt learned of the incident.

There were many other incidents resulting from my grandma's helplessness as a blind woman. She was a feisty, stubborn old lady but I was her favorite and I loved her. I would listen to her true stories and fairy tales during bed time. She wanted me to live with her but my mama did not want to part with her youngest daughter.

Grandma Lina often rewarded me with trinkets, clothes or money after a task was done. So one day, when she asked me to slaughter a chicken for dinner that night, I could not refuse. I had never killed a chicken before. I considered it abhorring and bloody, but there was no one else to do it. I reluctantly sharpened a bolo, (a long wide bladed knife), then grabbed the chicken by the head. I put a bowl under its head to catch the blood. With both eyes closed, I cut its head with a back and forth motion. The poor creature cried aloud. I was crying with it. I released my hold when finally, it went limp, shivering its last breath before it died.

I was still weeping when my grandma came groping into the kitchen. She sensed my misery and put her arm around me. "Sweetie, I should have that operation after all, don't you think?"

Gardening

Gazing at the bright sun through the drapes of my bedroom window, I said to myself. "It must truly be spring now. Time to put away winter clothing, don on light working clothes, grab the rake, pitchfork, hoe and shovel. Put on garden gloves and hat."

As I ventured into the warm sunshine today to start my yearly ritual of gardening, I thought of my family of long ago, toiling, sweating under the hot sun from early morning to noontime, continuing after lunch and brief siesta, then resume until twilight time. As a child, I delighted in joining my family at the farm and tending to my small patch of kale, lettuce, tomatoes and green onions.

There is no Spring, Fall and Winter in my country of origin, so planting and harvesting continued all year round depending on the harshness and/or duration of the inevitable monsoon rains. The southwest monsoon season would start on the last week of May and on to December or early January, then the northwest monsoon followed in a couple of months in a regular pattern.

Without a doubt, my love of gardening had been shaped since early childhood. Wherever I lived, I did some gardening, or if it was not possible, I sought other places to enjoy others' gardens. During trips, domestic and abroad, I would always marvel at nature's gifts of flowers and verdant foliage. Once, I was nearly left behind by my co-excursionists at a temple garden in Tokyo, Japan when I lingered longer at the pond, which was surrounded by tall ferns, varieties of beautiful flowers in full bloom, well-trimmed shrubs and dwarf trees.

When I lived in New York for 22 years, I maintained a backyard garden of about 12 by 18 yards, large enough to make four to five plots. We put a vinyl fence around it to keep our dog from trampling on the vegetables. I had eggplants, varieties of tomatoes, cucumber, squash, basil, green onions and peppers. The climbing vegetables, like string beans and cherry tomatoes were planted along the side of the fence.

Joe, my deceased husband loved tomatoes so much that he would eat them while he was picking the ripe ones. He had them in every meal. We never had to buy vegetables during the summer and part of the fall seasons. We had abundant harvest, much more than we could consume, so I would give some to our neighbors and brought a basket to my office for my colleagues.

I had varieties of annual and perennial flowers around the house too. At the height of summer, our surroundings were a delight to behold. Zinnias, marigolds, petunias and gardenias were my favorites since they were easy to grow and maintain.

Here, in Del Webb, Sun City, my lot is not as big as I would have wanted, but there is enough room to plant some vegetables in my small backyard and flowering plants along the sides and front of the house. I plant most of my vegetables in plant boxes and the flowers in pots in order to avoid weeding, a chore which has become more difficult for me. Also, in this way, I could move my plants inside when it gets cold and then back outside when it is warm again.

People do gardening with different purposes: to spend leisure, as a hobby, for home consumption or for commercial purposes, for enjoyment and personal satisfaction. It is also a good exercise and is an excellent stress management activity. For me, the satisfaction I derive from gardening outweighs all the other benefits. Perhaps, this is because planting and gardening tend to keep the legacy of my family going. I had a well, closely-knit family, bound together with unity and devotion to work. Planting and gardening provided my family closeness and love and oneness, from the farm to the dining table where we shared and enjoyed eating the products of our hard work. There couldn't have been a more satisfying and more rewarding benefit of gardening!

My Pet Pig, Lino

When I was young, every morning on waking up, I would look out the window of my bedroom, the smallest among the four bedrooms in our farm house. The reason for this habit was to check on Lino, one of our dozen pigs.

Lino was only 6 months when I chose him to be my pet among his three brothers and two sisters. He was so lovable and cute. We had three dogs, 2 cats, a carabao, (a buffalo-like mammal) and countless chickens but none of them was more dear to me than Lino. He seemed to share my devotion too by letting out a loud "Oink! Oink! every time he would see me approaching the pig pen. When I would turn away to go, he lets out another "Oink! Oink!" louder than when I was coming. My heart would go out to him. When there was no school, I would sit at the corner of the enclosure and play with Lino until I was called for breakfast.

I would insist feeding the pigs although it was not my assignment. Mine was to collect eggs from the laying baskets inside the chicken coop. My sister and I, the one next to me, would often bicker because she said I was not following our work schedule. My mother intervened and prevailed on me to stick to my assignment. She said I was too young (5 years old) and was not strong enough to carry the pails of pig feed, a mixture of corn hash and water. I relented but spent more time with my pet after my chores.

In our farm, no one was exempt from work. The younger did the lighter tasks and the older the harder ones like, planting and harvesting the crops such as corn, rice, sweet potatoes, cassavas, peanuts and others, extracting the meat from the coconuts and drying them, fetching water from the spring and washing clothes in the river.

One day, I became sick and was bedridden for three days. My mother took good care of me, but I was unhappy because she would not let me go out to see Lino. I cried and cried until my mother promised that my father would take me to the pen when he arrived from work as policeman. Although tired, my father carried me to the pen on mama's insistence. I begged to remain with Lino until I became very tired.

After my emotional conversation with my pet, Papa carried me back inside the house. I was weak and tired from petting Lino, but I was happy. My talk with Lino went like this: "My dear Lino, how I've missed you! I said tenderly, petting him with both hands.

Lino: "I missed you too, Oink! Oink! Oink! Where have you been?" I was ill. I was thinking of you all the while." "Oink! Oink!, Grunt! Grunt! "I thought you had left me." Me: "Leave you? I would never do such a thing.'

Grunt! Grunt! Thank you for seeing me today." Love you! "Love you too!"

The following day, my papa took me to the pen again. He did not have to carry me. I was feeling so much better. He opened the gate so I could play with Lino inside. I noticed that Lino was not anxious for my petting, as he always was. He recoiled when I tried to hold him. "What's the matter, Lino?" He demurred and struggled to get free from my hold.

I held him more tightly and cradled him like a baby. Then, I felt a whoosing sound and a warm something penetrating through my pants. It was accompanied with a strong, awful smell. I screamed as I realized that he just did "it" on my lap! Lino jumped off me and ran to the other side of the pen. My father saw what happened and he laughed so loud, prompting my mother to look out the kitchen window. Both laughed heartily.

But I was not laughing. I was angry with Lino, but I quickly acknowledged that my pet had given me a hint by refusing to be cuddled. I ran to the river close by and washed myself up, feeling angry with myself. My mother joined me with fragrant soap, towel and fresh clothes. She said that the new feed affected some of the pigs including Lino.

A day before our Town Fiesta in December, when Lino was about three years old, my mother sent me to the store in town two kilometers away to pick up something. She told me not to hurry. Maybe I would like to look inside the new Clothing Shop? I could get something nice. She was extra amiable today, I thought. I happily did as she suggested. It was almost an hour before I got back home with a nice printed skirt and a pair of slippers.

There were two people with my father busy doing something at the side of the house. I saw a big vat over a makeshift native stove and I smelled burnt hair. Curious, I went to see what they were doing. They were skinning a pig! My heart raced! When I could not see Lino inside the enclosure, I instinctively knew that it was him they were preparing to roast for the Fiesta. (Festival)

I cried hard and refused to eat dinner that night. I did not eat the lechon (roast pig) during the next day's dinner either. I could not bear to eat my loved pet Lino. My father went to the next town the following day and got me a female piglet, which he hoped would console me. Its chances to be slaughtered he said was remote since she was to be used for breeding. I was comforted a little, but I felt that my beloved pet, Lino was irreplaceable.

Freedom

As we celebrate Memorial Day, Independence Day and other National Holidays, perhaps we should ponder on the meaning of freedom more deeply. The word has become a byword of many, is more frequently said and passed on, sought after by countless individuals, but has become so common that we tend to forget the true meaning of the word to each and every one of us, free people.

Freedom is illustrated in more ways than one. When a child learns to walk for the first time, he/she tries to free himself/herself from the mother's hold even if he is uncertain and falling is likely to happen. When that child becomes a teenager, he wants to be independent of his parents, to be free to do whatever he wants.

For the adult? Freedom means differently to different adult individuals. For instance, he/she wants to be free to choose a career, whether to get married or not and to whom, to seek more adventure or to stick with family. Today, there are many choices and alternatives, countless opportunities and chances to further one's ambitions, and many adventure venues available to everyone. But, ironically, there are much more discontent, dissatisfaction, problems and conflicts during these times than during the days of our great ancestors, when freedoms were limited. What is the role of freedom in these conditions?

Ask the poor of the poorest, hungry person what he wants. The likely answer is, freedom from hunger and want. An abused individual would want to be free from her abuser, and the prisoner wants to be free from the confines of prison walls. The righteous man of extraordinary talents and abilities aims to be free of rebuke, antagonized or of being a victim of envy, and a writer strives to be liked and respected and free of criticism. Refugees and asylees flee from their countries of origin to be free from deprivation, oppression, war and persecution. Many lost their lives, livelihood and property in the pursuit of the freedom, not merely to exist, but to live free from fear.

The young soldier ventures into war without the certainty of ever returning home alive in the precious quest for liberty in distant, foreign land to free unfortunate, oppressed peoples, leaving family and everything he holds dear. Freedom and liberty are often costly and elusive. History books detail wars and conflicts throughout the world involving both the victors and the vanquished with common goals: power, freedom, justice and peace.

To become a part of the free world is a common goal of many peoples of the world, even more precious for the less fortunate, the people who are captives of poverty, cruelty and injustice, constant apprehension and fear of their safety and comfort in their own places of birth. The struggle for survival and for freedom is more intense where they are wantonly abused or disregarded. Precious freedom! The pitiful cry of the abandoned and the downtrodden, the pride of the free!

And yet, do we, in all honesty value it as we should? To some degree for others perhaps, but disrespected and ignored by a lot more. Winning freedom is a prize, a cause for celebration. However, the once coveted and much sought after prize loses its magic and enchantment after a time for some people. We tend to forget that once we had dreamed of freedom and fought hard to achieve it. Are we now drowned by so much freedom? In one of his articles, Bishop Fulton Sheen said,"The more we indulge in the pleasure, the more we diminish the pleasure."

There is some kind of freedom that matters more than any kind of freedom. It is something that is hard or impossible to fight against and win: ourselves. Our selfish desires, our constant cravings for the material, discontentment, our blind ambitions and unsound judgment, etc. hold us captives for life. It is ironical, but aren't we ourselves and our frailties the root causes why so many lose their freedoms to exist and enjoy this world? Let's think about it.

Fact Versus Fiction

Thought for today by Tom Clancy: "The difference between reality and fiction is that, fiction has to make sense."

First let me point out the similarities between the two literary classifications. Both require creative imagination and skill, must be original and innovative. Both call for the ability of the author to generate and maintain interest in his/her story, poetry, novel or other forms of literature. Both have an underlying objective among others, to compel the reader to read on. Perhaps the difference lie in the way non-fiction and fiction literary pieces are being told. As one writer put it," They are really just another way of telling a story."

In my perspective, true or non-fiction as the name implies must be true accounts of events backed by true experiences, by research findings or by other authentic sources. Biographies, autobiographies, memoirs, know-how books, travel books and articles, personal, business and political documents and others are common non-fictions. Whichever types they are, they must be accurate, reliable, credible, and subject to verification.

Non-fictions are meant to instruct, to inform, to establish, pass on some important facts, to provide guidance, directions, etc., or merely to share one's experiences. On the other hand, fictions are meant to entertain, to provide fun and enjoyment, to satisfy a reader's curiosity and fondness of certain types of stories, to humor or evoke fear, or to challenge one's creative imagination, etc. There is no limit to one's imagination and creativeness. Both writer and reader share similar paths in trying to know or decipher what and how things happen and what comes next. Both live in the world of make-believe. Fiction writing offers and explores a vast and unlimited field, beyond any writer could ever cover. Unlike non-fiction, fiction does not normally need verification, query or authentication.

Fiction centers on the world of fantasy and make believe, taking the reader into a world of his/her own. Often, if compelling enough, fiction makes the reader feel like being a character in the story, the protagonist, the antagonist or a supporting character. The skillful fiction writer can either make the reader laugh or cry, fearful, get angry, deep in thought, pause and wonder, expects more to happen, or exclaim with disbelief and other mixed reactions. When these effects happen, the story is a success and the story writer shall have accomplished his goal. They also reveal that some fictional stories, essays or novels are as near to reality as possible and that they make sense.

Buddy, My Buddy

My first dog when I was in New York, Misty, died of old age. I was so heartbroken that I did not want to have another pet any more. Three days after Misty's death however, I found myself in an animal shelter, looking at the selection of dogs of various breeds. I took fancy on a black and white one month old Labrador mix immediately. She looked so cute and was separated from the others. I was told she was just brought in and needed to adjust before mixing with the others. I decided right then and there that she was the one for me.

I named her Lassie because she looked like the character in the movie entitled "Lassie." I enjoyed Lassie, a quiet, lovable dog for thirteen years. I took her with me when I moved to Huntley in 2007. By then, Lassie was much older and sickly too. I got another dog from the Huntley Animal Shelter for her replacement in case she died. She passed away after I got Tinsel, a two month old female Beagle. My daughter thought Tinsel needed a companion, so she gave me one of her three dogs, Buddy.

Buddy is a male, white, Sitsu/Terrier mix and was three months old when he joined my household. Buddy's story was sad. He was thrown into the sidewalk from a passing car of a heartless owner in front of Vanessa's house, my daughter's friend working in the same hospital with her. Vanessa took him and they had him for a while. The husband did not like pets in the house, so although Vanessa and the children loved the dog, they gave him to my daughter.

Buddy is a barking dog. He would bark at the mailman, at the newspaper deliverer, the garbage collector and at anyone who gets close to the house, much more at anybody who visits. He is a very good watch dog. But that is not why I love him so much. He is my real buddy, loyal, sensitive to my attentions and seems to know what I am up to. I am even inclined to think he reads my thoughts too.

For instance, he knows I am going out when I go into my clothes closet and pick out a dress to wear. He watches me when I am getting dressed, putting on simple make up and brushing my hair. He even stays around when

I am in the bathroom and knows when I am done. He follows me all over the house and does not sleep until I sit down on the couch to rest. He would lie down beside me on the couch and sleeps at the foot of my bed every night. I have to tell him where I would be in the house at a particular time, because if I don't and he does not see me, he howls mournfully. He knows when I am going on a vacation and watches sadly when I am packing.

Buddy is sensitive to even the slightest sound. Early one morning before I got up, I sensed that he was very restless. He sat up suddenly then jumped down the bed. He came to my side and nudged me as if trying to say something. He paced around my bed back and forth, agitated. I did not hear anything but when I opened the door of my bedroom, I heard a very tiny pinging sound. It came from the carbon monoxide alarm. It had run out of batteries. When my smoke alarm went off one day, Buddy went crazy. Thunder and lightning make him crazy even more. In all of these, my other dog, Tinsel is never affected. They differ vastly in their reaction to stimuli.

There is one thing the two of them behave in the same way, however. When I arrive home from a vacation, it is always a very happy reunion for us. Both dogs would jump all over me at the door, kiss me all over and cry dogs' cries as if they truly missed me as I have missed them. They seem to understand everything I say. If only they could speak too!

I don't think I could go on without my beloved pets. They are more than pets, they are like family members, even closer than family. Many dog lovers share this view. I can't leave for extended vacation times. I love them both so much, especially Buddy. He is more attached to me and me to him in a very special and endearing way. He is my true buddy in the real sense of the word.

A Father's Promise (A Tribute to Fathers) Fantasy

"Are you going out fishing, Carl? "Elsa asked her husband anxiously while Carlos was putting on his old jacket and tattered hat. "Of course, dear. This is the first night of the squid fishing season. I cannot miss my first catch." "But the weather looks bad. It could be rough out there in the ocean." "Don't worry, darling. It could only be passing showers. The monsoon season is over now."

Carlos went over to the other side of their nipa hut where his three children, Lito, 16 Joanna, 12 and Lucy, 8 years old were doing their homework. He put his youngest child on his lap, gathered his two other children around him and said lovingly: "My dear children, wait up for me. I am going to get those delicious squid for our late dinner. We shall have squid for dinner every night throughout the season. How do you like that?" He kissed each one tenderly.

"May I go with you, father?" "No Lito, get on with your homework. I shall be home before you know it. I shall bring home the biggest catch you would ever see." To his wife, he said, "Keep the fire burning, dear. Lito, get more firewood for your mother."

After kissing his wife, he let himself out of their shanty, whistling as he went into the gathering gloom. Outside, the full moon was obliterated by dark, ominous clouds.

Carlos was pulling in his catch when a flash of lightning streaked across the ocean sky. He glanced at his basket and saw that it was almost full of squid, their thin skin, luminous in the dark. He let out a contented sigh as he pulled up the boat's anchor. His family will have a feast tonight, he thought happily.

He was still far from the shore when lightning flashed again, followed by a deafening thunder. Heavy drops of rain started to fall. Soon, the ocean became a blur. Carlos could not see more than a couple of feet ahead of him. He paddled on across the mounting waves, unsure of his direction. Suddenly, a giant wave swallowed up his hapless boat. Carlos fell into the angry sea. He struggled for some time, fighting for dear life until he could struggle no more.

"Is father home yet, mother?" Lito asked stifling a yawn. "No dear, but keep awake, son." "Mother! Mother, we are scared of the lightning and thunder! Where's father?" The two girls clang to their mother in fear. "Hush girls, your father should be here soon. Get back to bed. I'll wake you up when father gets home." As Elsa rekindled the fire in their native stove, she peered outside worriedly. The rain seemed to intensify every minute and the wind was blowing ferociously. She crossed herself when another lightning struck not too far from their shanty. She did not sleep waiting for her dear husband's return. But Carlos did not come back home.

When Elsa went out to their porch early the next morning, she saw a basket full of fresh squid sitting on the landing. "Carlos!" She called excitedly. She looked everywhere in the house, went outside calling his name but Carlos was nowhere to be seen. Elsa asked her neighbors to help find her husband. They searched around the house, the beach and beyond. The futile search was abandoned after several days. Carlos was never found.

However, every morning throughout the squid season, the family would find a basket full of fresh squid on their porch. In their hearts, Elsa and her children knew who caught them. They ate the mollusks with tears in their eyes. During the next two years of the squid season, the basket full of squid kept on coming.

Lito quit school and learned to fish to support his family as his father did. On the first night of squid fishing, Lito had a big catch. Standing on the bow of his boat facing the ocean, Lito cried out aloud. "Father, you have fulfilled your promise. Thank you, my loving, dearest father! I am taking over from now on. Rest in peace now."

The basket of fresh squid ceased to come from then on.

The Lady in White

Sitting on an aisle seat, third row from the front, at St. Mary Catholic Church on a Saturday morning, I had a good view of the Bridal Entourage as it started to march along the aisle to the front of the full church. As the "Here Comes the Bride" was played, I watched the colorful procession, focusing on the beautiful bride in her glittering bridal gown, her radiant face under a veil of white, embroidered tulle.

When I turned towards the altar following the entourage, my eyes caught the face of a young, beautiful lady dressed in white, seated directly opposite my pew. She was also wearing a white veil, which made her look like a bride herself. Was she one of the bridesmaids and was late for the procession? I found myself focused on this girl who stood out among the guests in her pew. I thought she looked sad when she glanced sideways to me.

When the priest pronounced, "You may now kiss the bride" part of the ceremony, I heard the lady cough, blow her nose followed by a low moan. At this point, I was sure that she was crying. For what reason? Curiosity assailed me and prodded me to watch this obviously distressed person.

At the end of the ceremony immediately followed by a Mass, I looked around to where the lady was seated. She was no longer there. Did she leave before the end of the Mass? I wondered.

I drove to Prairie Lodge, Del Webb, Sun City to attend the Wedding Reception at the Drendel Ballroom, following a stream of guests' cars along Kreutzer Rd. To my surprise, I found myself seated next to the "lady in white" at the banquet hall. "Hello!" I said. Hi!" she retorted absentmindedly. Her eyes were focused on Robert, standing with his bride at the entrance to the Banquet Hall. I wanted to strike a conversation with the lady but I decided to respect her brooding silence.

Dancing followed immediately after dinner, started by the new couple, followed by their relatives. I danced with my friend, Delia, Robert's aunt and then with Marc, Delia's boyfriend. The lady remained in her seat mostly alone. When "Moonlight Serenade" was played, I urged Marc to dance with the lady, but she had left the table before Marc could ask her.

At a friend's birthday party in Schaumburg the following Sunday, I was leafing through a photo album when I came across a close up photo of a smiling couple, sitting close to each other, holding each other's hands. They looked familiar.

"Susan, who is the lady in this picture? I asked my friend, the birthday celebrant.

"That is Louella. She died instantly from a car accident on 1-90 two years ago. The accident happened three days before her wedding with Robert." Susan bowed her head in sad remembrance of the tragic accident.

I was speechless. So that was Louella, the ill-fated bride, the "lady in white." Susan was too busy with her other guests to notice my discomfiture.

That night, I lighted a candle for the tragic lady in white. I think she had chosen me to pray for her. "May she rest in peace." I prayed.

Enchanted April

"Push! Push!" The midwife urged Angelina as she held the pregnant woman's knees to keep them open and upright. It was her second day in labor. Angelina's brow was puckered and her perspiration flowed down her face and neck faster than the midwife could wipe them. She closed her mouth firmly and pushed as hard as she could again and again. Nothing happened.

"We have to take her to the hospital. I can't continue with this without risking Angelina's life and the baby's. Please call the ambulance." Rey, Angelina's husband who was watching helplessly was on the phone before the midwife could finish her sentence. Shortly, the sound of the ambulance' sirens broke the morning's silence in Digos Village.

At the hospital, the stricken woman was wheeled instantly into the delivery room. A nurse handed Rey a sterilized gown at the entrance, but Rey declined to go inside. He could no longer bear to see his wife in great suffering. If only he could take away her pain or bear it for her. Rey agonized. He went outside to the veranda and took out some cigarettes. He recalled the year prior to his wife's pregnancy as he puffed on his cigarettes one after another.

He and Angelina had been married for 10 years but they could not have children. The couple left their businesses in Digos, Davao and went to Manila to see a well-known gynecologist. They were told that something was wrong with both of them. The treatments they received failed to yield positive results. They flew to New York, USA and consulted with two more gynecologists at Presbyterian Hospital and at New York Cornell University Hospital. They underwent more sophisticated treatments. However, all efforts by the world-renowned specialists were in vain. The couple's condition could not be remedied.

The exasperated couple went back home and consulted with a quack doctor living in a distant village, known to cure rare diseases and remedy childlessness. The old quack doctor advised them to attend a séance. "Great Asena!" He called out. Hear my plea for this couple!" The séance group did not hear the rest of the quack doctor's plea. A mighty rush of wind shook the whole house. It put out the three lighted candles on the table. The group huddled together in the semi-darkness, terrified.

That night, Rey had a strange dream. In it, he saw a beautiful lady whose face was as radiant as the full moon. She had long hair, which touched the floor. "Bathe with your wife in the stream behind your house at the crack of dawn tomorrow. Do not wipe your wet bodies. Let the water dry by itself. In a few months, your wife will become pregnant. The child is going to be the most beautiful girl you would ever see. I will allow you to keep her until she is eighteen years old. Only until she is eighteen! The lady repeated in a louder tone, then she vanished as quickly as she had appeared, leaving a thick smoke behind her.

"Congratulations! Mr. Ramirez! Your wife just delivered a very pretty baby girl!" Rey was interrupted in his reverie by the excited voice of a nurse. His wife was smiling happily although she was still weak and sleepy. A big celebration was held at their hacienda (large estate) attended by the whole village three days after the child was born.

Rey did not tell his wife about his dream. He did not want to spoil their joy. They named their adorable baby, April, Angelina's choice as she was born on a bright April day. During April's birthday each year, they would get a most unusual gift, a basket full of wild flowers that stayed fresh all year round. It was the same sort of basket, white, with gold trimmings around its side, but different varieties of flowers every time. Their scents were of rare perfume and lingered until April's next birthday.

On the night of April's fifteenth birthday, Rey's wife asked him. "Where do you think these flowers came from, dear? Rey was speechless for a while, thinking of an answer. His wife asked the same question each year. "It probably came from a secret admirer," he finally said as convincingly as possible. They left it at that. Angelina did not bring up the subject again. But Rey was worried. He recalled the strange lady's words in his dream. Was it true? Is their daughter going to be taken away from them when she turned eighteen years old? "No. That would never happen," he vowed.

After the girl's sixteenth birthday, he spoke alone to his wife. "Darling, I would like us to move from here to a distant country in Europe, somewhere remote, quiet and safe."

"But why? This our home. Our daughter is very happy here. I am happy here too. Aren't you?"

Rey told his story, the story he had kept for so long." Nonsense, Rey. I would not hear of it," the wife replied vehemently. In spite of his wife's objections, Rey sold all their properties and businesses, including their hacienda where they lived since they were married. Very early one morning, before their daughter turned eighteen, the family boarded a transatlantic flight to West Germany and settled in a picturesque valley in the peaceful village of Stuttgart. They had bought a villa at the edge of the village bordered by hills. April was made to understand that they were there for just a vacation. She was always an obedient, lovable child and never questioned her parents about anything.

On the night of April's eighteenth birthday, which they celebrated quietly at home, the couple heard a conversation inside April's bedroom. April's voice was loud and angry, but the other voice was calm and soft. Rey and Angelina rushed to her room. They found the door bolted from the inside. Rey took a chair and smashed the girl's bedroom door. They were just in time to see their daughter floating up through the ceiling and into the dark nothingness outside. The couple was utterly surprised and overwhelmed with the strange happening right before them. They held each other, weeping. They finally slept, overcame by extreme distress in the wee hours of the morning. They were awakened from their fitful sleep with a voice, the same voice Rey heard in his dream years ago. "Do not be upset. I have only taken what belongs to me. April was never yours to keep." Then, silence.

"Mama! Papa! Goodbye!" They heard their daughter's plaintive voice, which faded into the dawn's ethereal silence.

Fear

I never knew real and constant fear until I worked and lived in Africa. It all began with the fear of the unknown and in the uncertainty of working in a distant country, far away from my beloved children and from the rest of my family who had always been there to help and protect me. There was also the nagging worry that I would be sick while there. Were there hospitals in the place I would be assigned to? Who would look after me? The fear also that my young children would get sick and mommy was not there to take care of them filled me with sad, gloomy forebodings.

Many other unhappy thoughts and fears almost made me give up signing my contract. Only two strong motivations compelled me to go ahead: to provide my children with a brighter future in the promise of good, better income, and to heal a broken heart caused by my husband's desertion.

Many challenges and dangers faced everyone, particularly with foreigners working in the Dark

Continent: Insect bites including poisonous snake, scorpions, spider bites, killer bees sting, etc. Wild animal attacks, hostile natives and cannibals in some areas were real threats. Infectious diseases abound like leprosy, malaria, tuberculosis, intestinal and skin diseases, and yes, Ebola, which they first named "Lassa fever" since it originated in a remote village called Lassa. This deadly disease was feared by everyone, natives and foreigners alike and for good reason. The person infected by it died in less than twenty four hours after the first symptoms. There was no known cure then. There were at least two in our batch of teachers and another in another batch who died of the disease, leaving us all in extreme fear and wondering, "Who would be next?"

In the north of the country where I was assigned during my first year, all the above were true except cannibalism, which the local people brushed off nonchalantly. They insisted that the cannibals lived in secluded, distant areas, far from towns and cities, living among their kind. But how would they explain the occasional disappearances of children and young adults? I wondered. My fear of these man-eating people bothered me especially when I had to go to remote, deep village schools to supervise Teaching Practice of our college students. Fortunately, I was transferred to a more civilized part of the country and my fears were alleviated, somehow.

Fear (continued)

Fear in the Moonlight

The kind of fear I am about to describe was truly terrifying, true and immediate, one I would pray will never happen to me again. It happened before I was promoted and reassigned to the southwest of the country from the northeast of Nigeria.

I was walking alone one moonlit night after dinner to the Needlework Room about five hundred yards from my house to supervise my students making needle craft projects. The moon was full but the brightness was softened by the shade from the tall trees along my path and from the bushes surrounding the Needlework Building. I had my flashlight ready in case the electricity would go off before I headed back home. Electricity in the college powered by generators was only for five hours, from six to eleven p.m., enough time for staff and students to have dinner and do supervised studies.

I was halfway to the Needlework building when I heard a hissing sound on my left side. A broken pipe? No. We had no running water. Someone following me? No. I was alone. I turned my flashlight on, focusing on the spot where the sound emanated from. About eight feet from me, a large, black and white snake was poised to strike! Its ugly face was fierce, its eyes were bulging and its long tongue was out, moving from side to side. The rest of its shiny body was coiled around the trunk of a tree like a rope.

I froze in fear, unable to utter a cry at first. I finally managed a loud scream in that wild, life-threatening second. My students responded instantly, brandishing sticks, stones and anything they could get hold of and shooed the mean reptile away. It slithered back into the woods at the rear of the building. It was a poisonous, deadly variety.

The frightful encounter left me a nervous wreck. For a couple of nights, I had nightmares, screaming and waking up in the middle of the night with a sweat. I developed a phobia for all crawling creatures, which I could not shake to this day!

The Psychology of Marriage

Why do people marry? Why do some who got married want to get out of it? And why do some do not want to get married at all? These are questions as basic as, why we eat and why some people do not like to eat certain food. Question number one is as old as the time people became more and more aware of the necessity of companionship, of intimate union or connection with somebody one desires or loves, to have a family, for convenience, or to fulfill an obligation connected with certain beliefs or tradition. Tribal, ethnic marriage rituals and arranged marriages are good examples.

Perhaps there had never been a time in history when two people can satisfy their longing for companionship, intimacy and love as easily and as conveniently as today. Couples meet, get connected with each other, get married or live together without the benefit of marriage, separate, then seek another person, get married again and part afterwards, or simply give up without trying again after an unhappy experience.

We see the advent and advancement of modern science and technology, taking away our youth from the love and comfort of home to the pursuit of independence and the thrill of internet discovery. The lure of travel and adventure, the constant movement of human kind to seek fortune and opportunities farther and farther away from home, leaving behind a loved one/ones oftentimes lead to break-ups and disillusionment. So many homes have been broken because ambition and the outside world beckon with blinding glitter too strong to resist.

Why marry? Why navigate a path, which has proven to be difficult or thorny to many through his own, through the partner's fault or both's fault? Sure, to many, marriage is still held sacred, a union that is binding and lasting to Christians and to other believers. "What God has joined together, let no man put asunder." This is only one of the many religious sayings so profound and soul-searching it could lead one back from where he/she had wandered from marriage, if the person has a soul, or at least believe in it.

Then again, why do some people do not want to get married? Is it their choice, out of luck, a disillusionment, fear of responsibility or failure that make them so decide? I have acquaintances and friends who are single who never got married, or got married but got out of it, got divorced, separated and never want to get hitched again. A few left their families for no reason and sought yet other partners. Still, some live with somebody of their own sex, get married and adopt children, or just go on together for financial benefits.

Why are all these relationship situations so complicated and anti-social? Is humanity so diverse, restless and unstable now? Or have we gone amuck? Where is the glorious past when people lived in simple and uncomplicated lives, contented with what they received and able to give, what they had and what they were?

But then, the skeptical would probably say that we do not want to go back to the primitive, to the past, which held no surprises and thrill, glamour and excitement. So, would you prefer to be married and keep it, seek other alternatives, forego with or forget it? Where are you now in the perspective of marriage bliss, or more lastingly, contentment, which is beyond happiness? In the scale of from 1 (lowest) to 10, (highest) what level are you in terms of this ideal state of marriage achievement? No one else could tell except yourself. That's human behavior and you alone can dictate and control it. Think about it like you would in choosing a career or making an important decision.

Marriage. Like it or not, it is an attractive proposition, but very challenging and nerve-wracking at times, sweet to behold, inspiring and appealing, but how is it going to be inside it? Sweet, or sour?"

An Interesting Personality

Lina is my first cousin's wife. I never really knew her well until I came to America, on my way back to Nigeria in 1976. She lived in Trenton, New Jersey and worked at Beth Israel Hospital, New Jersey for many years as a staff nurse, then as a supervisor.

Being my first visit to the country, she toured me around New Jersey's attractions, to the beaches, to the casinos in Atlantic City, the Boardwalk and other notable places, and introduced me to her close friends. She became my tour guide, visiting New York, the Big Apples' tourist attractions like the St. Patrick's Cathedral, the Museum of Natural History, Central Park, Rockefeller Center, and walked with me along the shopping centers of the elite on Madison and Fifth avenues. She took me to the Statue of Liberty on Liberty Island, on a ferry boat, cruised with me around Governor's Island and showed me the complicated subway system.

She gave highlights of each place with accuracy and enthusiasm of a true tour guide. She made me feel relaxed and confident in her company. She explained historical places like an authority and moved about, entirely sure of herself. It was with reluctance that I left to continue the rest of my trip back to Nigeria. However, we remained in contact with each other through letters.

When I decided to live and work in America in 1985, after my contract in Nigeria ended, we were both delighted to be reunited. By then, she had petitioned her six children to become residents, who subsequently became U.S. citizens. I took the subway and then the path trains from Manhattan to Jersey City, New Jersey, where she would meet me at the station. This became a routine every weekend when I was off work.

Lina was always active, vivacious and knowledgeable. She would talk about any topic under the sun with a kind of enthusiasm that was catching. Ask her about politics and she would engage you like she was a politician, or about diseases and medicine and she would talk like the doctor herself or the pharmacist.

She could talk incessantly but she would never bore you because there was always a touch of humor in her dialogue. She was charming and witty, still is, even now in her mid-eighties. The topic she loved most to discuss with wisdom, sincerity and reverence was the Bible. I found it amazing that she could quote Bible passages off hand, including chapters and verses. Perhaps her ability and skill in discussing the Bible passages are more accurate and precise now since she is engaged in many activities in a parish in Houston, Texas where she lives now. She is the head of Catechists, Bible Study instructor, a church volunteer and is active in parish events. I would not be surprised if I hear more of her engagements.

We had been together on a cruise to Alaska in 2008. I fully experienced and shared her deep faith and devotion to the church during that voyage. There was no mass she and I would miss on board ship. In many ways, we were compatible and right for each other's company. I consider her the most interesting person I would enjoy to spend my time with in any circumstance, at any place.

Thoughts I Had on a Rainy Day

Have you ever heard of the monsoon seasons? These usually occur in southern Asia, characterized by heavy rains, strong winds and thunderstorms, pretty much like the hurricane seasons that originate in the tropical areas of the Atlantic Ocean.

The monsoon seasons in my country are of two types, the southwest monsoon and the northeast monsoon. The former occurs mainly from late May or early June to December or early January, and the latter from early

February to May or June. When these seasons are really bad, homes get blown off, bridges get carried away by strong currents from swollen rivers. Roads become impassable due to flooding and homes in low-lying areas get inundated or destroyed completely. Schools, businesses and events get cancelled for days depending on the impact and duration of the season, disrupting lives and livelihoods. Lives, human and animals are lost, injured or incapacitated.

When it is raining in our area, I think of one bad monsoon day in my country, when I was in my teens. The heavy rain and wind started during the first day of our Fiesta Day, (festival) in December, a major annual event. This special day was (still is) celebrated with much fanfare, marked with parades, crowning of the reigning queen selected through money as well as beauty contests, playground demonstrations, participated by High School students and Elementary pupils and contingents from all the barrios. There were outdoor and indoor movies too, band-playing contests, a lot of dancing and dancing contests and music. Every house prepared sumptuous meals, featuring a special fare we call Lechon (roast pig.) and everyone was welcomed, invited or not. Celebrations lasted for three days. Guests from out of town flock to our town to enjoy all the fun, the food and merriment.

Our farm house was battered by the strong winds and heavy downpour throughout the day and all through the night during the first two days of the event. Our guests of a dozen men and women had to remain in our house until the following afternoon when the weather subsided a bit. My poor mother and sisters never stopped cooking and serving food to our extended guests, and in keeping them as comfortable as possible. Our house looked like some barracks, filled to more than its capacity with people occupying every space of our dwelling. It practically became a campsite or shelter. The general mood was somber instead of festive. When the guests could leave finally, they were profuse with thanks to my family. We were left with some feeling of relief and a sense of satisfaction for our deeds of kindness and hospitality.

The rains continued to fall intermittently for about seven days more. That was even lucky because monsoon rains could last from nine to ten days, varying from area to area, making life miserable for both men and beasts. I was particularly sad that time in December. I had looked forward to go into town, two kilometers from our home, where all the happenings took place. My friends and I were going to watch the dancing and calisthenics field demonstrations on the first day, ball games and singing contests the following day, movies at night and ballroom dancing on the last night.

Instead, I was marooned inside the house, restless like a trapped animal. The endless pounding of the rain on our rooftops almost drove me crazy. My thoughts were not of a girl of thirteen, but of an old woman bent from a heavy burden, nursing gloomy, unhappy thoughts.

A Tale of Love and Despair

Joel (RIP) was an apprentice in a Philippine Interisland vessel operating in the Manila/Visayas route and I was graduating from college when we finally met after writing to each other for two years. The meeting was arranged by my closest friend in college, his town mate, who was responsible for our pen acquaintance.

That first meeting was unforgettable, exciting! We hugged, speechless, filled with joy and longing for each other. There was no need for words in a while. We felt we had known each other for the longest time and were reunited after a long separation. Through regular exchange of letters from my end, radiograms, telegrams and letters from his ports, our love developed gradually and developed into a beautiful, long distance love affair.

We could not wait any longer. We had a grand wedding after my graduation that year. He had finished his apprenticeship and was now a Third Mate officer of an interisland vessel. We had our honeymoon on his ship. The captain gave up his cabin for us as a wedding gift, while he conveniently took a leave. We would spend our evenings after dinner on deck, and sang together accompanied by his guitar under the pale moonlight that illumined the calm, smooth sea offshore around the Manila Bay with its glorious sunset. The days were spent also on deck, trying our luck on fishing. When it rained, we would stay inside ship, listen to music or play cards. Each moment we spent together however way they were spent were precious and passionate.

Ours was a blissful marriage, bursting with love and never-ending romance, interrupted only when he had to go back to his ship. Each parting was agonizing, each reunion a celebration, a renewed sweet honeymoon. Such was my life as a sailor's wife. But I was very happy with the love we shared in spite of his constant absence. In fact, separation made our hearts grow not only fonder but intensified our affection for each other. We never quarreled or disagreed about anything. There was no time for discord.

Each moment we were together was precious and endearing. We hang on to each other dearly and passionately as if our existence depended it. During six years of marital bliss, we had three adorable children, a girl and two boys. Joel was not only a loving husband but a doting father to his children. He pampered us with gifts he would get from different ports, watches, jewelry, clothes and home décor, etc. He rose steadily from third mate, to second mate, to first officer, and finally, on our seventh year of marriage, he became a captain (Master Mariner.) Eventually, his routes abroad on ocean-going vessels resulted in prolonged separation, from three months to five months in a row. Meanwhile, I was a very successful teacher, a loving mother and a happy contented wife.

Then, the winds of change started to blow. His letters, which came regularly previously and radiograms became more and more scarce until they ceased to come. I sensed gloomy foreboding, intuition? Not long after, through reliable sources, I learned that he had fallen for a tour guide in Singapore, his home port. What happened to love that seemed so perfect?

Despair tore my heart into a million pieces. The sleepless nights, the miserable, empty days weighed heavily on me. I went down from 115 lbs. to 80 lbs. My children had sustained me, thankfully for them, and kept me from falling over the edge. They became like unwavering pillars holding me up to face the stormy skies bravely and stoically. Family and friends began to inquire about my husband. I had to invent plausible excuses, that he was in Europe or in another continent and would come back soon to get his family. An employment offer abroad was a blessing in disguise coming at the right time, when I was running out of excuses for my husband's prolonged absence.

Working very hard in a foreign, distant land became a balm to my aching heart and lifted my ailing soul. Seven years of loneliness and struggle for survival in a strange land full of dangers, life-threatening situations and challenges dragged on slowly. The going was very tough, testing my level of endurance almost to its limit. My children whom I had petitioned to join me strengthened and prodded me to go on, yet again. Bless them!

Then, far from my expectations, the captain surfaced from his exile and sought to be reunited with his abandoned family. Through my sister in-law, we became a family again. I was too hurt to accept him back, but my children were too happy to have a daddy again that I relented. Children after all do not harbor hate, only love.

He joined us in Nigeria and remained for three months, trying his best to make up for the years he had abandoned us like nobodies in the wayside. He again became the same doting, loving husband and devoted father. The dying ember of love was rekindled, aflame with renewed passion. But he was still under contract with a Greek Shipping Company in Singapore. So although his employment with the Lagos Maritime Co. was more or less secured, he had to go back to Singapore to complete his contract for three more months after which time he vowed to be as close to his family as possible.

But he never came back. He was accidentally stabbed when he intervened in a fight between two of his crew.

Because it happened two miles from shore in Colombo, Sri Lanka, no immediate help was available. He died of massive hemorrhage before he could be brought to a hospital in town.

Despair visited my poor heart once again, a despair more acute than the first as it was a final, ongoing one. It was more devastating to feel despair and loneliness in this way, than when you felt heartbroken when abandoned by someone whom you knew was alive somewhere in this world.

Love is a torch that lights up and lift the spirit; Despair blackens and sends it into the dark abyss.

My Favorite Places

There are many places I would like to be and stay. Let me group them according to the changing seasons. In the fall, for instance, I would like to be in St. Lucie, one of the exotic islands in the Caribbean. That lovely spot in Castries, a beach resort with a long stretch of white, sandy beaches, the beautiful rugged cliffs lining the shoreline, and where just above the shallow, aquamarine waters, the proud seagulls flirt with one another incessantly, are more than enough to entice one to tarry longer. A picturesque, lush mountain lay silently and imposingly in the background, as if guarding the merry crowd frolicking in the crystal clear water. The majestic Caribbean mountain loomed in the distance across the bay, framed against the cloudless, blue skies. The sailboats that seemed to outrun one another provided wholesome entertainment. The wide expanse of the blue ocean was calm, serene and smooth like silk. It was a picture perfect panorama worth the whole day viewing and the lovely place worth going back to again and again.

In winter, I would like to go back to my small hometown in the south of the Philippines, where no changing seasons prompt the change of clothing, moods and routines, etc. I would sit under a shady mango or coconut tree and write a poem or story as I savor the sweet smell of ripe pineapples or jackfruit filling the air with delicious fragrance. The singing of lovebirds perched on the bamboo tree nearby would be my background music. My long, lost happy childhood would be the theme of my composition. When tired of writing, I would pick the ripe, luscious guavas that abound around the farm. While I munched on them, I would try to relive the unforgettable, glorious past haunts with my siblings more than 60 years ago.

In the summer, I would prefer to remain here in the U.S., where my thirty years stay had taught me many lessons of adjustment, satisfaction and disappointment at times. The changing seasons have become more natural to me now than they had been when I first came. Summer is as enjoyable in this country as in many other countries of the world I had visited. The possibilities for fun and enjoyment are endless, whichever part of the country one chooses to go. My deceased husband, Joe used to say," You like to go abroad. Don't you know that there are many places in the U.S. more beautiful than those you see in other countries? Indeed, "America, the Beautiful!" Americans are more blest in their homeland and in many ways than others may think.

Springtime! It is undeniably the best and the most preferred season of the year. European countryside in the spring is gorgeous and awesome. Trees, picturesque mountains, hills vying in their height and beauty, tiny lakes, flowers everywhere in the backyards and gardens and on window boxes, seemingly beckon and enchant the passersby. Europe is exceptionally beautiful and classically enchanting. I would not hesitate to live in one of those colorful villas along Lake Zurich, with views of the Swiss Alps in the far distance, in historic Sorrento or romantic Capri, Italy, in the beautiful valley of Stuttgart, Germany, or in any of those villas, adorned with the inevitable wind mill surrounded by magnificent, colorful tulips in Holland. The choice is limitless.

However, I would probably stick to our own endowments. I would go back to Vermont, to Martha's vineyard, or to Virginia in the spring. Seeing and enjoying all these places and many other attractions would want one to proclaim that it is grand to be alive, to rejoice in the wonders and beauties of the world.

Although some people would like to be in Northeast of the country during autumn to enjoy the fall foliage, I would like to see the rolling hills, the small rivers that snake their way across the valley and the caves that held many secrets all over again in historic Virginia and in all the other places I had the pleasure to visit. In spring, as the rest of creation emerge from the onslaught of winter scourge, the snow, it is heavenly to inhale the freshness of grasses in the meadows and prairies and see the trees awakening slowly from their winter slumber. Most of all, I would love to watch the buds of flowers responding to the herald of the spring rain.

So What Do I Do Now?

Indecision is obviously caused by the infinite alternatives available to us from the simplest and least significant to the more complex issues. It is a persistent, common human behavior, or is it a weakness? Is it merely a result of our fickleness, or our dependency on others to answer the all-familiar question, "So what do I do now?"

Imagine yourself sitting at your kitchen table, or at a restaurant, wondering what to have for lunch. Your freezer or refrigerator is full of cooked food, or the restaurant menu is laden with many favorites. Which one to get? To cook the best dinner for your picky husband, Salisbury steak, beef stew or pot roast?

How to deal with a friend you have wronged or offended, apologize or not? Then there are more complex issues like buying a new home. Where? Which type? Where? Move to a warmer climate in the south, Florida, California or Texas? Still, a more painful and excruciating dilemma, to separate from or divorce a husband of many years who is making life miserable for you and for your children, or to stick it out through thick and thin? Which school or college to send your children, or with whom to spend retirement, with one of your children's family or live alone on your own? How would you spend the lonely days ahead? The issues go on and on: What do I do now, how should I do them?

I had faced that question an awful lot of times in my lifetime, from choosing a career, where to apply for a position after college, where to reside after marriage, how to survive when a family tragedy struck, whether to sign a contract for employment abroad and leave my beloved children behind for some time. They all involved difficult decisions to make. I had surmounted every problem quite satisfactorily on my own through sheer determination and of course, through my strong faith.

My deceased second husband Joe was the most kind, most generous, most independent-minded husband a woman could ever wish to have. I never once heard him ask," What do I do now?" Decision-making did not seem a problem for him. In fact, he gave me the liberty to choose the alternative best for us under certain circumstances, and he never complained of the result of my decisions, sound or not. Blame game was not his style, either.

He knew I loved to travel, so he would consult the Travel Section of the local Sunday paper even before reading the front pages, and pointed out the places I might want to go. He did not like traveling but he never prevented me from going to any place. With his help, choosing a place to visit was in itself, a pleasure, instead of a hassle.

When he died of COPD in 2007, naturally I was devastated. Who would now help me with the what, where and how? Do the shopping, write checks, do other errands, do a million more things for me as he used to do? I was suddenly faced with the inevitable question, "So what do I do now? The question has been popping up more regularly now since then.

Indecision! It is a crossroad many do not want to go through, but it is always a pathway to navigate unless one has enough fortitude to just hang his/her head and take or leave it.

Auras

1. My College Professor

Quite a few people have aura about them. Perhaps it may not be discernible readily and fleeting at the first glance to some. However, there are those whose special qualities are perceived instantly at first sight, or in a moment's association or acquaintance. It is something that is difficult to pinpoint and to describe and as such, only the highly perceptive could notice. Aura is a part of a person's appearance, an involuntary behavior or demeanor, without necessarily the person's effort to display awareness of her gift.

It is an inherent gift in a person, a unique charm.

I perceived this pervasive quality in one of my professors in college, an interesting instructor of Greek Mythology. She was not breathtakingly beautiful, but there was something about her, a magnetism that would make one look at her twice or even many times. I could not take away my eyes from her as she spoke, and she spoke not only convincingly, but with a certain wit and charm.

I found myself anxiously waiting for her to walk into our class twice a week in her high heeled shoes which seemed to barely touch the floor as she walked. I would stare at her, watch her every move and hang on to every word she had to say. I regretted for the one hour she was with us to last. I was so struck by this lady's charm that I named my first born, a girl, "Paz Cielo" after her, which means "Peaceful Sky."

Aura No. 2

The Church of the Holy
Sepulcher, Jerusalem, Israel

In one of our shore excursions during a 13-days cruise to the Holy Land, we visited many holy sites, one of the holiest of which was the Church of the Holy Sepulcher. The place was always full of visitors/pilgrims from all over the world, starting from the gate to the Walled City, to the entrance to the church itself. It was a daily sight of anxious and pious people who did not mind the huge impenetrable crowds, who braved the sweltering heat and humidity to get a glimpse of the Holy Sepulcher in the interior of the edifice, where the Holy Jesus was laid after His Crucifixion some 2000 years ago. There was hardly elbow room as we struggled our way towards the church under the scorching midday sun. By the time I finally reached the entrance to the church, I felt I was going to collapse from sheer exhaustion. As I entered, all worn out but happy, the figure of Jesus laid in the Sepulcher on the mosaic wall greeted me and filled me with an indescribable, compelling urge to continue to gaze at His dead body in the arms of His Blessed Mother. Seeing the tomb where Jesus was actually buried, preserved in its original state, made me weep. The whole place evoked an "aura of holiness," an unexplainable atmosphere and mixed feelings of deep emotion, an overpowering awe and wonder that resulted in a deeper faith in Him, Our Supreme Creator who died on account of our sinfulness.

The fatigue I felt before I entered inside this holy place entirely vanished, replaced with euphoria, an extraordinary, rare feeling. That was the best, rarest "aura" I had ever experienced that will linger in me all the days of my life.

The Sea and Me

The farm house where I was born in was only two kilometers (about 1 and ½ miles from the sea. During low tides throughout the full moon, the sea would recede a mile or so off the shore. My three older sisters, 12 to 6 (me) years would go down to the sea to gather seashells that were exposed on the dry sand: clams, sea urchins, edible seaweeds, crabs, mollusks, shrimps and other varieties of soft and hard bodied seashells. The tide would stay low for an hour until the end of the week when it gradually rose sooner. We picked whatever sea shells we could find and headed home before the tide came up again. My small basket would not be as full as my sisters' but I did not mind. The fun of being at sea was enough for me. I loved the smell of the sea. I would take time from shell gathering, inhale the ocean air deeply and gaze at the ocean beyond, wondering what its deep waters held in its mysterious depths.

When I was ready for college, I traveled by ship from my province south of the Philippines to Manila and back home during vacation times. The two days at sea each way were filled with creative thoughts. I was inspired to write poems about the sea, an amateur's work, which I promptly discarded. That was not the end of my fascination with the ocean. In fact, it was an ongoing fancy that climaxed when I married a marine officer.(Love of course was the prime factor.)

We had our honeymoon on his container ship. It was a wondrous time for me, not only because I was married to a most loving and romantic husband, but because I got a closer, intimate rendezvous with the sea as we navigated back and forth from Manila to other harbors across the channel. My husband would take me to the open deck after dinner and we would sing together with the accompaniment of his guitar under the starry night as our ship glided smoothly on the calm sea. The famed sunset over Manila Bay was a heavenly sight, more so because I shared it with someone I dearly loved, on a setting I enjoyed, the ocean.

I missed the ocean when I worked in Nigeria, West Africa. Job as well as family took precedence over my original passion. When I immigrated to New York much later on, my second husband, Joe and I would dine at restaurants in Howard Beach, or at other eating joints along Sheeps'Head Bay in Queens. He also loved the ocean, having been in the Navy during World War II. My move to Illinois from New York after Joe died was a sentimental journey. I sought solace traveling, mostly by sea.

Cruising with great ships to exotic, exciting places to many corners of the world was a happy reunion for me with the ocean in its vast, awesome splendor. Relaxing on sunny white beaches, riding in open carriages along surfs and coves, swimming in pristine, shallow waters in the Caribbean, Waikiki Beach, Bermuda, etc. during shore excursions were endless fun. Walking on the ship's promenade decks while the ship continued its course, leaving behind white foam on the ocean's surface in its wake, viewing the ocean through the dining room's glass windows, or from the open deck buffet restaurants during mealtimes sharpened my love of the sea.

The ocean will continue to intrigue, amaze and amuse me, perhaps more than else could. Discoverers of ancient worlds had navigated the treacherous oceans to unknown destinations with great anxiety and fear of their fate. Now, we discover the world crossing the oceans with more confidence, safety, comfort and fun. I discovered more of my world through my passion of the sea. Its enigma continues to challenge me, its varying depths, its mysterious beauty beckons and prods me to go on flirting with it. There is something in it that keeps tugging compellingly at my restless nature, like a lamp attracting the moth.

Lamps are meant to be lighted but they get extinguished and moths fly away when lights are off. My friend, the sea would always be there, but I may not be able to answer its irresistible call again, not because I do not love it any longer but because there is always a period in every life story and a finale to every beautiful sonata.

I Can't Believe You Said That!

In October, 2010, I went on a 13 days cruise to the Holy Land with Rhonda, a 78-year old widow and her daughter, Jennifer, 42, a nurse at Woodhull Hospital, Brooklyn, New York. They were two of my closest friends with whom I went on trips before I moved to Huntley, Illinois. They lived in Queens with Jennifer's' boyfriend, Matt, whom Rhonda disliked.

We reserved a stateroom on the 11th deck on Equinox, the largest Celebrity Cruise Lines ship at the time. It had a balcony and automatic front and bathroom doors, ideal for Rhonda who had three knees and hip replacements, diabetes, high blood pressure, high cholesterol and a heart condition. She needed a walker when inside the cabin and a wheelchair when going out.

The ship had a contraption in one swimming pool, which would lift and come down for the disabled to dip into the pool and get up unassisted. They also had other amenities for the handicapped, like preferential seats in the restaurants, in the theater, in the library, in the internet room. Helpers were available to push the disabled passengers' wheelchairs around the deck of the ship.

Jennifer and I joined the shore excursions in every port while Rhonda remained on board ship. Although some handicapped passengers went to shore excursions on wheel chairs, Jennifer did not like pushing her mother in a wheelchair around the rugged and hilly terrain in Nazareth, Jerusalem, Galilee, Ceasaria and Jordan under the sweltering heat. I offered to help so that her mother could see the places of interest, but the daughter was adamant in leaving her behind.

Mother and daughter argued a lot, from what time to eat dinner, which restaurant to eat, which theater shows to see and lectures to attend. Rhonda loved to attend the health lectures and participate in the sitting exercises. However, I sensed that she was unhappy about her mobility problem and in being unable to enjoy herself fully, which was understandable. I refrained from discussing the fun we had during our shore excursions for obvious reasons.

On our third day in Israel, Rhonda insisted joining us to an excursion to the Church of the Holy Sepulcher in Jerusalem to see the burial site of Jesus. They had a heated argument. Both were getting more angry as the argument continued.

"You are impossible!" Jennifer shouted at her mother who was now crying. You should not have come with us!" Between her tears, Rhonda shouted back at her. "Throw me overboard! You and your good for nothing boyfriend would be happy without me!" Exasperated, Jennifer threw her hands in the air and said aloud. "I can't believe you said that!" Then, she marched outside the room, slamming the door hard behind her.

Dread

One morning years ago in Abeokuta, Nigeria where I worked as Education Officer, I woke up with a gloomy, mysterious foreboding, a powerful tug sending unexplained shivers on my spine, akin to fear that something was about to happen or just happened. The feeling of dread persisted throughout the time I was still at home getting ready for work. The uncanny feeling disappeared in the middle of a busy work day in the college.

After work hours, it came back again. I could not remember feeling that way before. It was strange, unwelcome and disturbing. What was it? I thought of my children in school. Were they alright? I drove to my children's school to pick them up with unusual urgency. I felt great relief when I spotted them emerge from the school entrance one by one.

I had entirely forgotten about the mysterious feeling a few days afterwards. The college where I worked was going to celebrate its first foundation day set in two weeks time. I became fully immersed in my department's (Home Economics) preparations to participate in the program of events for the much anticipated day. There were meetings with my staff and checking the students' progress in finishing their projects for the department exhibits. Rooms for the displays had to be cleaned thoroughly and repainted. As Head of Department, I had to see to it that everything was in place in every detail. We were expecting prominent officials in town and high officials from the Federal Ministry of Education in Lagos as guests throughout the two days event.

I was too tired to pick up my letters from the mailbox in the main building one afternoon after an exhausting day. I sent one of my two boys to get them. He was waving a yellow envelope as soon as he got inside the house. "Mommy, Look! The college secretary said I should give this telegram to you at once," he said excitedly. My heart raced as I opened the envelope. It was a message from my husband's corporate office in Singapore, an awfully sad news:

"Capt. Joel R. Amar died on Saturday, April 24th. He was stabbed by accident when he intervened in a fight between two of his crew." Reply ASAP. Signed, Capt. George Greenwald, In Charge of Operations, Singapore Pacific Maritime Company.

The blow was very hard for me and for my children. We were inconsolable for the longest time. He had planned to move to a Maritime company in Lagos to be close to us when he finished his company contract in three months. His abrupt, untimely death altered everything. Then, I remembered the dread I was feeling a few days ago starting on the 24th of April. So that was it, a subtle premonition of a tragic happening!

My Favorite Movie

I have always been fond of romantic movies. In fact, I like love stories regardless of their genre, and whether they are in film, in print or related verbally.

One of my favorite movies is, "An Affair to Remember," a romantic classic. This film one would surely remember and maybe not forget, a poignant love story, was nominated for four Academy Awards in 1957. It is a cinemascope picture presented by Twentieth century Fox Film Corporation. It was written by Leo McCary and Mildred Cram. Leo McCary directed the movie himself.

An affair to Remember is opened by a love song of the same title, sang by Vic Damond. The main protagonists are Cary Grant who played the handsome gigolo, Nicky Ferrante and Deborrah Kerr, the stunning nightclub singer, Terry McKay. Cary Grant is my favorite actor, and Deborrak Kerr, my favorite actress.

The setting of the story is an ocean liner bound for the port of New York from England. In the movie, both Nicky Ferrante and Terry McKay are engaged to be married. Their fiancés are waiting for them to disembark in New York. They fall deeply in love during the voyage. Before their ship docked, they agree to meet at the top of the Empire State Building in Manhattan and get married in six months time.

The rendezvous does not materialize because Terry McKay was hit by a car crossing the street to their meeting place. In the meantime, Nicky was waiting for her at the summit of the Empire State Building from 5:00 p.m., the agreed time until midnight, notwithstanding a thunderstorm. The accident results in Terry's incapacity, but she chooses not to tell Nicky about her misfortune. Ken, Terry's fiancé is a very patient and understanding man, standing by Terry in her miserable state of affairs. Terry finds a job when she gets well at the local parish school as a music teacher to young parochial children.

During all these time, Nicky Ferrante does not marry his fiancé, an heiress to $600 million fortune. He works very hard as a painter, which he is very good at and sells his paintings through the help of a friend. His most beautiful portrait of a beautiful lady, Terry McKay herself, shows her wearing his grandmother's Spanish lace shawl. His grandmother who was 82 years old, died after the two had visited her at her beautiful villa in Sorrento, Italy during their shore excursion. She had left word to give the shawl to Terry, whom she liked very much after she died.

Without Nicky's knowledge, Terry visits his gallery and purchases her own portrait, from Nicky's friend at a much lower price because she does not have much money. Nicky's friend also takes pity on her because of her physical condition.

Nicky has been wondering whatever happened to his beloved Terry. At the height of his longing to see her again and find out what happened to her, he finds himself wandering in the city streets, thoughtful and brooding. One evening during Christmas, while he is leafing through the telephone directory, he comes across her name and address. He decides to see her before he sailed out of the country that evening.

He is ushered into her apartment by the housekeeper. Terry is sitting on a couch by the fire, speechless at his sudden appearance. All throughout their conversation, Terry remains reclined on the couch. She makes no move to stand and shake his hands, which prompts Nicky to suspect that something is wrong with her. Putting two and two together, he comes to a dramatic conclusion. He then opens the door to her bedroom and there, hanging on one wall is Terry's portrait, which he had painted.

The love struck couple embrace and kiss, both realizing that no accident could come between their immense love for each other.

Why I love "An Affair to Remember? 1. I am romantic at heart, so much so that most of my book collections are romance novels, same with my DVD's. I guess I could be called "an incurable romantic." 2. The plot of the story is very realistic and effective in generating a sense of loving and in loving unconditionally, and in being happy to receive love in return. 3. The story has a little humor in it, breaking the monotony of continuing drama. 4. The flow and sequence of the story is continuous, not fragmented.

Last but not the least, I like the main characters very much. How they dressed and looked, the way they spoke and acted. It is very classic, not vulgar. The settings and scenes are attractive and inspiring too.

Lottie

It was a fine, early spring morning. I was doing my usual chores in the kitchen when I heard bird cries. They were small but sharp and sounded frantic. I continued my routine. I have become used to hearing bird chirping around my backyard, on my veranda and on the two trees in the front and side of the house during the onset of spring and throughout the summer.

The cries continued and was becoming more faint and weak. I opened my front door and looked around. I saw two birds perched on the tree close to the veranda. They were jumping from branch to branch of the bare tree restlessly but they were quiet. Meanwhile, the cries continued. This time, I decided to find out from where the pitiful cries came from. From the garage area!

I opened the garage door and looking up to one side of the entrance, I saw a small brown bird inside the lamp holder. The poor creature was trapped inside. It made louder noise as it saw me, as if pleading for help. It was trying desperately to get out of its temporary cage. How did it get inside the lamp enclosure? I tried to reach the lamp holder and its prisoner, but since it was too high for me, I grabbed a step ladder and reached for the bird inside the cage. It was scared at first and tried to avoid my probing fingers, but when I held it gently and got it out, it relaxed in my hand.

"Hello, little starling, how did you get into trouble?" I held it with both hands gently. "Let me see. I'll give you a name. I pondered for a second and came up with a name." Aha! Lottie! That's what I'll call you, a name synonymous to "little." Do you like it?" I came down from the ladder and settled in one end of the couch inside the garage with Lottie tenderly but securely capped in my hands. He or she (How to determine its sex?) I knew not, looked quite pretty. It also felt weak but alert. It probably was worn out from the prolonged crying for help. I felt sorry not to have rescued it sooner. The bird looked at me pitifully, as if pleading to be released.

Suddenly, two birds swooped towards the garage, flying back and forth at the entrance then alighted on the roof of my parked car. Its parents? No doubt. I held little Lottie closer and whispered to her." I hate to see you go, my little friend, but your parents would like to take you home." I released my hold and immediately, Lottie joined her parents. The three birds flew out together, leaving me with some regret, but on the other hand, a feeling of relief for the family's reunion.

A week afterwards, I heard loud chirping outside my bedroom window. When I looked outside into the backyard, I saw three birds perched on my vinyl fence, gleefully jumping and chirping. Saying "thank you," and perhaps 'goodbye?" My heart went out to these humble creatures who obviously came back to show gratitude. I never saw them again after that.

Premonition

I was born and grew up in a country which clings to certain customs, traditions, beliefs and superstition. They are tied up with our cultural habits and practices to this day. The advancement of education and the advent of science and technology did little to change our legacy handed down from generation to generation by different countries.

During the colonization era, the Turks, English, Portuguese, Chinese, Spanish, Japanese and then the Americans, left imprints on our emerging culture. The Spanish who remained in our country for 300 long years had undoubtedly influenced the Filipino culture and shaped our ways of life more than the other colonizers had. Most likely, we got our belief in "premonition" from them.

"Premonition." The sound of the word evokes fear and anxious foreboding for me. My mother used to tell her young children many stories about strange dreams and manifestations, which she perceived and believed as preludes to sinister, unfortunate or unexpected happenings in the foreseeable future. Consequently, all of us in the family (especially us, six young children) grew up with a firm belief in premonitions as inevitable, unavoidable forecasts of impending doom or disaster. Premonitions hang over our heads like the proverbial "Sword of Damocles," to fall anytime on our lives.

I had three experiences with premonition that linger in my mind to this day. The first was before I went to work in Nigeria in 1975. In a dream that I had before I even applied for an education officer position, I saw tall trees, bushes and hills bounding a deep valley. A small river ran along the middle of the village dotted with mud houses. I experienced extreme loneliness and isolation living alone in a tiny bungalow exposed to all dangers: snake bites, disease, etc. I did not think of that dream until I arrived in a remote village northeast of the country, my first station. Strangely, the place looked exactly as I saw in my dream. I mentioned this place in my previous story.

The second premonition was when my first husband, a captain of a ship based in Singapore had a fatal accident at sea in April, 1983. He was accidentally stabbed when he intervened in a fight between two of his crew. I was getting into my car to take my children to school one morning when I found my car filled with large flies. How they managed to get into the car when all the windows were closed was beyond me. The following day, a telegram about the devastating news of my husband's death in Singapore, Malaysia came.

The third premonition was in August, 2003, when my older sister, my favorite among my siblings was struggling with terminal ovarian cancer. I was pressing clothes in the basement of our home in Queens, N.Y. one evening when suddenly large flies came buzzing around the room where I was doing my work. All our doors and windows were tightly screened! How they got inside the house was again puzzling.

We were already fast asleep that night when the telephone rang. It was a long distance call from my niece in Manila, informing me of her mother's death a few hours earlier. I had already more or less anticipated it. The flies foretold the sad event.

I truly believe in premonitions based upon my actual experiences, from the tales my mother used to tell us and from other people's accounts. Accidents, death, other misfortunes happen and many if not all are preceded by some kind of warning, unusual manifestations through sudden presentiment, a sense of foreboding or "gut feeling," as others call it. Some people have more keen perceptions and become anxious of what may come. Others are skeptical, or do not even take notice of the signs.

Somehow, we are foretold of the inevitable. Is it God's way of telling us to be prepared?

Moonlight Serenade

As I reflect on the above title, I cannot help but feel nostalgia for my childhood days in my small town, south of the Philippines some 65 years ago. Serenading was then a common practice, so much a part of courting a woman in our town and in other towns as well. We had inherited the custom from our Spanish forebears. The young men did their serenading the beloved with much enthusiasm and fervor to the point of competing with one another in singing and in playing the guitar and other musical instruments. They would usually go in groups of two, three or more. Sometimes, the determined suitor would go serenading solo although rare.

They would serenade more often during moonlight nights as there were no street lights to light their paths when the nights were dark. Neither were there cars to get them from one place to another. If the lady sought after lived in a far barrio (small village), they would trek to her place when there was no moon carrying torches, navigate the rugged terrains or cross rivers or streams, ride on a boat up and down the river, and climb a hill or mountain if they had to. Nothing impeded the smitten young suitor from his pursuit and in letting his devotion known to the beloved. There were still other challenges that the avid admirer had to face to compete with the other suitors.

Who was the best singer? Who could play the guitar or other instruments best? Was the suitor good looking? Was he well-off? Did the girl care for him? Was he liked or favored by the girl's parents? The latter was a very important consideration. Parents had their final say during those days. If they approved of the suitor, the serenaders were invited inside the house, were served with drinks, snacks or dinner and they were encouraged to continue their singing and playing their instruments inside the house. On the other hand, if they did not approve of the man, they were shooed away by the father or mother of the girl, or ignored.

I remember a scenario clearly when I was about ten years old. My mother liked my oldest sister's suitor Prudencio very much, the son of a wealthy family who lived in a far town. The father was the Mayor of their town. Not only did my mother invite the group inside when they came to serenade my sister, but she went out of her way to make a special dinner. She also offered the group of three lodging for the night since they lived far away. My sister eventually married the man with my parents' full blessings.

An opposite scenario took place at another time. My mother did not favor the suitor of my other older sister, the third in a family of six. (I was the youngest daughter.) She was the prettiest among us sisters and the smartest too. The man was the son of a city councilman but my parents disapproved of him because he was not good looking, jobless and a drunk too. When he came serenading one night with his friends, my mother took a bucket of water and hurled it into the serenaders below. The singers dispersed hurriedly and never came back again. That was mean, but it was a common practice during that time.

There were instances when lovers defied the parents' wishes. After nights of serenading and there were no favorable responses from the parents, the lovers eloped. As a result of their disrespect and defiance, the couple got cursed, was not allowed to enter into the girl's household again and denied inheritance. This same story happened to my mother and father.

My father's fault was that he came from a very poor family, whereas, my mother's family was rich and influential. Never mind that he was good looking, kind and soft-spoken gentleman and a good musician too. His traits did not count as far as my mother was concerned. Apparently, my father was not good enough for their beautiful daughter, who was sought after by many other better suitors. But my mother loved my father and him, her. That was enough. They eloped one night!

When I grew up, I had many suitors too, even in my young age. I went to Manila to pursue my college degree and whenever I would come back to my hometown during vacation times, young men serenaded me almost every night. Did my parents approve of any of them? Did I choose one of them?

No, is the answer to both questions. I went back to Manila to pursue my Masters Degree in Education after my mother died and settled in the city. Sadly, there were no serenaders in the city although I had relentless suitors, one of whom swept me off my feet. He was never a serenader but he sang in my heart so sweetly and so passionately that I forgot all about serenading and serenaders.

"Moonlight Serenade!" my favorite classic instrumental piece that was often sang or played during my prime days! And those soulful serenades! Gone are those memorable serenading days forever!"

First Impression

"So what do you think of Angela, mom? "My son Clyde asked me after he had taken back Angela to her apartment after our dinner together. Angela was a doctor, a General Practitioner from Romania, working as resident physician at a hospital in northeast Miami, while my son was an engineer and computer analyst.

"She is very pretty, but isn't she a bit serious? I did not see her smile even once during our dinner. She does not talk a lot either, does she?" I said hesitantly. "Oh, she was just shy meeting you for the first time." My son did not say anything more about the girl he was going to marry.

During and after their wedding held in Las Vegas, I observed the same demeanor in Angela as the first time I met her. After three days in Las Vegas, they continued their honeymoon in Hawaii then settled down in Miami, Florida. I did not see my son and my new daughter in-law again for several months after their wedding.

My first impressions of my son's wife were of being distant, deep, hard to fathom and uncaring. These impressions prevailed and was heightened when she would not call me, and when I called them, she would give the telephone to my son after just a few greetings.

In 2006, my husband Joe was diagnosed with COPD (Chronic Pulmonary Disease,) a year after my son and Angela got married. After months of going back and forth to hospitals, his condition was declared terminal. Clyde and Angela came to New York to see Joe and remained with us for one week. During that period in time, I saw a different Angela. She became more communicative and open and caring in her tone. More pleasing to me was the way she called me "mom." There was some hint of affection in the way she spoke to me. I was a little surprised as well as delighted with the transformation.

Most admirable was the way she fussed around Joe. She stayed with him at the hospital and observed the way the hospital staff took care of their patient. Of course, out of professional etiquette, she did not interfere with their job. After a week when their leaves of absence were over, Angela took me aside and said sadly. "Mom, Joe is going anytime now. I would advise you to call Hospice Care." She hugged me and continued in a more sad but professional tone. "You have to be strong. We shall be back as soon as my leave and Clyde's are renewed. Clyde has to postpone his job-related trip abroad as well. Take care."

After they had left, Joe's condition turned for the worst. I brought him back to Queens General Hospital Center of N.Y. again but his doctors told me the same as what my daughter in-law had said. There was nothing more the doctors could do for my husband. I called my children in Miami and told them of Joe's near death situation.

At the hospital, Angela took over the whole situation. She introduced herself to Joe's doctors, conferred with them and arranged for an oxygen tank for Joe. Being a Saturday, it was difficult to obtain an oxygen tank, but through Angela's persistence, we got it. Angela contacted Hospice Care and we took Joe home on his insistence. He would not want to be in an ambulance, but to go home in his own car. Angela held Joe all the way home from the hospital. My two sons carried Joe inside the house, while my daughter held the oxygen tank. I was too distraught to do anything.

That night, Joe showed signs that he was going to pass on. "Mom, it's time to call the priest," Angela urged me. After Extreme Unction was administered by our parish priest, Joe's condition improved. My children and grandchildren headed back to Miami except my daughter who is a nurse. Every day and every night, Angela called to follow up. Joe finally passed away four days after he was brought home from the hospital. At the wake and during the funeral, Angela never left my side. Throughout this difficult time, she was very caring not only for Joe but for me. My initial impressions of her were proven wrong.

I have heard of other people's first impressions that turned out untrue. Some of my previous first impressions also turned the opposite either for better or worse in many instances. Whatever happened to first impressions, which are said to be lasting? Or am I quick in my judgment, skeptical, lacking in the ability to discern the other person's character or good qualities during first or brief encounters? One consoling thought is that, I am not alone in this regard.

If I could Live Her life

"It is truth universally acknowledged that a single man in possession of a good fortune must be in want of a wife." Such is the opening statement in Jane Austen's literary masterpiece, "Pride and Prejudice," expressed by the main protagonist, Elizabeth Bennet.

Jane Austen is one of my favorite authors, whose life was simple but respectable, as indicated in her biography attached to the book above. I enjoy reading the novel and I have seen its movie version in two volumes many times. I became so fascinated with the movie that I ordered its two volume DVD so that I could watch it over and over again whenever I like. The main characters, Elizabeth Bennet played by Jennifer Ehle, and Mr. Darcy played by Colin Firth, were well presented.

I like the character of Elizabeth Bennet as portrayed by her famous creator both in the book and in its adaptation in the movie of the same title. She is charming, witty, independent, and a lover of nature. She was the father's favorite among five daughters. I wish I could live Elizabeth's life, especially when she finally married Mr. Darcy, a handsome and wealthy gentleman of noble connections, whom she hated at first.

But since she is only a fictional character, I focus on her creator, the celebrated author, Jane Austen. She was born in Hampshire, England in 1775 and died from a form of lymphoma in 1817. Although she grew up during major political and social upheavals in England, she had based her novels not on those conditions but on her personal experiences and observations. This is particularly true in her novel, Pride and Prejudice.

Although her biography does not specifically mention it, I surmise that many elements in this classic novel were true happenings in her life, including being a member of a large family living in a countryside manor among the gentry. Her attendance and participation in country dances and balls, roaming the countryside and enjoying nature's endowments, extensive reading and playing the piano were common in those parts during that time among young, beautiful girls from decent families. In my perception, Elizabeth Bennet is a reflection of Jane Austen's character in many ways.

If such is the case, I wish I could have lived her life, seemingly peaceful and stable, although she never got married for some reason, or be like her character in Pride and Prejudice whose qualities I admire. Most of all, I wish I could be like the writer that Jane Austen was, timeless and universally acclaimed.

What I Wish to Accomplish

Several ideas come to mind at once while I contemplate the things I would like to do this year. For a starter, I have to continue writing my fourth novel, a romance/ fiction set on a modern cruise ship sailing the high seas. I have postponed writing momentarily during the busy Christmas and New Year holidays and resume full speed ahead during the coming four months, with the hope that it will find its way to the publisher by June or early July.

I traveled outside the country only once in 2013, a cruise to the Bahamas with my oldest granddaughter, a gift for her 16th birthday. In June, this same year, I plan to visit my home country, the Philippines to attend a reunion with my school mates residing abroad who are also coming home. I should be abroad for three weeks, the maximum time I could be away from home because of my two dogs. Keeping them in the kennel or with a dog sitter are very expensive.

En route to the Philippines, I plan to take a one-way cruise to Tahiti and New Zealand, places I have not been to yet, and then proceed to Manila by air. My main destination, my hometown, Lopez Jaena where the reunion would take place will be the last in my itinerary. I am also planning to celebrate my next birthday on June 19th at my beloved place of birth, something I have not done before since I left home 60 years ago.

In the fall, I intend to join a tour of several states and cities within the USA by rail. I am quite tired of traveling by plane or by sea. Railway travel offers an entirely different travel experience, safer and more relaxing. It would be refreshing to view the countryside on board a modern, comfortable train. The fall foliage is glorious in October, especially in many states in the northeast. Amtrak Vacations offers vacation packages, including hotel stays and guided land tours during this season.

The months of November and December are going to be devoted to attending several events and functions within Del Webb, Sun City and at other places, depending on what the winter weather would allow. I would also start writing my fifth book, an Epic/Romance novel set in my province, Misamis Occidental during World War II in the Philippines. More readings and researches would demand much of my time writing this book as it would include a lot of historical episodes.

There are endless things to be accomplished in this life. One does not need to put an effort to find and do them. Retired people like me have more time to do anything worthwhile that takes their fancy such as leisure activities they could not do during their working days. We do not lack time now, we only need the determination to fill our time with things we wish to do that were postponed before, satisfying and rewarding endeavors, not necessarily for purposes of monetary remuneration.

Confessions of a Travel Nut

Are you a travel nut? Well, I am. I' m a very enthusiastic, zealous and fervent lover of travel. I guess I had already shown my love to "go" ever since I learned to walk. My mother used to tell me that I had fallen many times when I was a baby. I fell down the stairs when my mother left me for just a second, from a window when I tried to climb out to go with my sisters, stumbled and hit my chest on a stone while I was running after my mother who did not want me to go with her to town.

I used to tag along with my sisters or with my mother wherever they were going, ran around the house, making my family crazy, walk around our big farm after school, roam the fields picking guavas, etc. And when I was in grade school, oftentimes I would be late home picking blueberries or mangoes along the way home.

"Nene, (that's what they called me), you run around like a chicken constantly looking for food." Can't you ever keep still?" My mother used to remark. "This girl will go places one day," one of my aunts predicted.

When I was in high school, I would not miss to join class field trips in town and in class excursions to neighboring towns or adjacent provinces. During open market days, I would go into town not only to do food shopping but also to have the chance to walk around with friends and visit others.

College was oceans farther from our town. I had to take a ship from the provincial capital to Manila. The trip would last for a week or longer during the bad weather. I loved those sea voyages, whether the sea was rough during the monsoon seasons or smooth as silk during the calm days in the summer. I would long for the vacation days when I had to go back to our town for the summer breaks, and looked forward to board the ship again to resume school work. I would love to watch the sea with the waves rolling gracefully as our ship would glide over its blue surface and count the sea gulls as they fluttered around the ship's bow. And when the ship dropped anchor upon arrival in its destination, I would regret disembarking from it.

Nigeria, West Africa

My passion for travel abroad began to be realized in 1975 when I was recruited to work in Nigeria as a contract Education Officer. To reach that country opposite the globe, the trip was long and arduous. The journey starts in Manila, four to five hours layover in Hongkong, China, Bangkok, Thailand or any other Asian City, onwards to any port in Europe closer to Africa, like Spain, Brussels, Belgium, Paris, France, Italy, etc. An overnight or a day stopover in any of these cities, then overnight flight to Lagos, Kaduna, or Kano, Nigeria, completed the journey.

My contract was for two years each tour, renewable at each end. It carried a lot of perks and privileges. One of the many was the opportunity to travel out of the country at the end of each tour for free. Every two years after renewing my contract, I would go to any country of my choice after visiting my family in the Philippines. I brought my children along with me during my travels. I had completed a total of six tours before I finally decided not to renew my work contract any longer.

I had seen most of Nigeria during my nine years work there, while giving lectures, speeches and attending conferences and workshops in different major cities and towns in the Federation. My experiences in that far-away country were a combination of hard work and pleasure as well.

My love for travel did not end there. I went home to the Philippines and remained for one year, after which time, I resumed my travels, then took up a position in New York with the Department for the Aging as Entitlement Specialist, Food and Nutrition Lecturer and Case Manager of four Senior Centers in Queens, New York. I spent all my vacation time from work traveling to various places in the country and abroad.

When I retired after my husband died in 2007, opportunities for travel increased. I felt I could not stop wandering around the country and around the world through cruises, land vacations, bus tours and train trips. I have covered almost the whole of the U.S. east, west south and north, Canada, Alaska, Bermuda, South America, the Middle East, the Mediterranean countries, Scandinavian countries, Northern Europe, the Caribbean islands, Mexico, Panama, Japan and Australia.

Of course, no matter if one travels every day, no one could ever cover the great expanse of the earth from end to end. Travel these days is very tempting and more and more attractive places beckon to the anxious traveler. In my advancing age, I feel I could still go on traveling. I intend to keep on going while I still can. That's the travel nut that I am.

What Difference Words Can Make

What would our lives be without words to communicate with one another? We would be like the first people on this earth who hardly communicated, and if they communicated at all, they probably used sign language, utter sounds only they could understand, or through actions to demonstrate what they meant to say. It had been for certain a very lonely, uneventful life that had no meaning, no importance and no memories to live by, to recall or pass on.

We have gone a long way since then. Now, words express our thoughts, feelings, desires and actions, even dictate our destiny. Words make writers, poets, orators, professionals, tradesmen, educators, etc. and "help politicians get elected." They inspire lovers, bridge distances, reaffirm and strengthen faith and religion. Its functions are limitless. They are indispensable tools, so important in everyday life, yet so commonly and loosely used and overemphasized that some do not appreciate their value any longer. Sometimes they are misused resulting in disharmony and discord. On the other hand, they could also inspire and unite people to rise up and proclaim success or victory.

They have become forgotten instruments, like old tools that are used frequently that their value is disregarded and no longer noticed by some. Furthermore, there are those who abuse or use words blatantly, wantonly, disrespectfully, even cruelly at times. It had been said by a philosopher that, "the arm can only stretch its length, but the small, boneless tongue can go an unlimited distance, even across and beyond seas."

Words, as used today by everyone can inform, convey and clarify meanings that can flatter or make another happy, can encourage or discourage, can fill one's heart with love, pity or anger, cause triumph or defeat, increase hope or despair, can fill one with dread, anxiety or with relief and a host of other human emotions and expressions. These expressions make people today vastly different from our primitive counterparts.

Sadly, some are inclined to use words without regard to the other person's feelings. "You mindless bastard! How could you do that? Or in a much better way: May I know why you did that?" "Shut up! Loud mouth!" Vs. Will you please be quiet?" "Move! Are you crippled?" Vs. "Kindly move a bit, sir/madam, thanks." "Hurry up! You move like a turtle!" Vs. "Can we speed up a little bit, please?" "Enough! You son of a… (expletive) Vs. "I think you have said enough." "I hate you! I never want to see your ugly face again!" Vs. "Maybe we should not see each other again."

There are many other incidents of misuse, unpleasant ways of using words. Uncalled for use of words in the concept of good manners and civility can be considered as verbal abuse. On the other hand, pleasing expressions seem to be disappearing from some people's vocabulary. "Sorry, Thank You, I beg your pardon, Please, If you'll excuse me," etc. are easy to say and to hear, and would go a long way to achieve a good purpose. It may be time to ponder on these wise words of wisdom by sages of old: Three most important words are, "If you please," two most important words are, :Thank you." And the least important word is, "I." Also, someone really thoughtful said, "It is better to say nothing if good cannot be said at all."

We all have instances of uttering improper words sometimes out of impatience, exasperation, of boredom, or in a fit of anger and disgust. Being only human is a common excuse. Perhaps there is always an excuse for sudden bursts of thoughtless and annoying expressions. When it becomes a habit, then it needs serious consideration. Or, we probably would be better humans if we go back to the primitive ways of life!

Christmas in the Philippines

Christmas in the Philippines is celebrated with a lot of fanfare and lasts from December 16 to January 6, the Epiphany (Three Kings). In my town south of the country in particular, the dawn masses (Mesa De Gallo) and Novena start at 4:00 a.m. and go on every day for nine days. The Solemn High Mass is sung in Latin by the church choir, accompanied by my father's band. All the townspeople who are Catholics (85%) attend these masses.

The culminating Novena and Mass are said at midnight on the 24th, Christmas Eve. The Bishop or Archbishop of the province would officiate the Solemn High Mass, joined by three or four priests from other parishes. Every household would prepare special native fares for their families and guests on Christmas Eve and for Christmas Day. Young and old people look forward to these events with feverish anticipation for the fun and joy the events bring: laughter and merriment, gifts, music and dancing, delicious food and endless local drinks. People from out of town partake of the free, elaborate festivities and food, invited or not.

Households who could afford prepare Roast pigs, we call "lechon." The pig is stuffed with lemon grass, salt and other herbs. Lechon is our traditional fare during fiestas and other special occasions and holidays, especially during Christmas and Easter. No special event is celebrated in our country without the signature Lechon. The animal is roasted slowly over live coal for 4 to 6 hours, depending on the pig's size. We used to raise pigs in our big farm. Some of our friends and relatives would reserve their pig with us well in advance of the events.

Caroling is so much a part of our Christmas rituals. After the first dawn Mass, people young and old would go caroling. They would sing outside or inside the house they visited and were given money or gifts and served food and drinks. The caroling continued inside the house if they chose to go inside, in which case, they carolers would also dance. They went in groups of four to six members and covered as many houses as time allowed. Sometimes the caroling would continue to the wee hours of the morning, particularly after the first dawn Mass.

I can still vividly remember as a girl of five when I started to participate in the caroling with my older sisters. Since I was the youngest in our group, people were fascinated with my singing and dancing. I would often get more money than my older sisters did. Our older brother used to chase me around the house, begging for some money from my night's earnings. We had a lot of fun, but hard work too. We sang until our voices croaked like the frog's, and danced until our feet ached. In the end, we felt happy and satisfied that we had spent the season in keeping with the tradition.

My sisters and I would buy new clothes and shoes and saved the rest of our income inside a hallow bamboo tube. We had no piggy banks. I did not stop participating in the caroling until I went to Manila to pursue my studies. Even grown ups from 16 to 20 years old participated in the traditional caroling practice.

On Christmas Day, Godparents give money or/and gifts to their godchildren, another common practice. Parents would usually choose couples who had money to be godparents of their children, for obvious reasons. My own Godparents were prominent persons in town. They would give me P10.00 pesos (25 cents in dollar currency) and gifts in kind, like clothes or shoes. These plus the gifts from my other Godparents made me feel rich!

Many events were lined up throughout the season such as dancing in the Town Hall, parades and contests. Other towns and barrios in the country have some other unique ways of celebrating Christmas handed down from generation to generation. However, similarities also abound and are still practiced to this day. We had inherited these practices from the Spanish Conquistadores, who colonized our country from the 1600's to the 1800's. Their legacy, which we consider the most important was Catholic religion.

Before they came to our country, we were Muslims. Each province was ruled by fierce warriors called Lakans or Lakandulas or Datus. Other influences the Spaniards had on us were the love of music, dancing, fun and festivities, our temperament and features, names of places and people, the love of adventure and the Spanish language.

Some of our local languages have Spanish derivatives. Many Filipinos can understand and speak Spanish. It is still one of the subjects taught in our schools today.

The Spaniards brought into our country different food staples, like rice, corn, farm animals, etc. The other colonizers, the Dutch, English, Portuguese, etc. who came to our country before the Spaniards did, left no significant impacts on our culture since they did not settle as long as the Spaniards did. The Spanish influence had altered or shaped our culture entirely. Many still prevail to this day, including the ways of celebrating Christmas and other religious and cultural events.

A Dog's Story

My name is Tinsel. I am a ten-year old tricolored, female Beagle. My grandma Lydia adopted me from Huntley Animal Shelter in Huntley, Illinois when she moved here from New York. She had another dog, a 14-year old Labrador mix, which she brought with her from Queens, N.Y.

Grandma decided to get another dog for Lassie's companion. When she came to the shelter, a worker brought in one by one, a Collie, a German Shepherd, a Sheep dog, a Terrier and me to select from. She spent only a few minutes with the Collie. The German Shepherd looked mean and frightened her, although he could be a good watch dog. The Terrier was a male. She preferred a neutered female. The sheep dog was a little too old. She wanted a younger, active dog who will replace Lassie should she die.

"Aha! So she was looking for a replacement for her old dog!" I could be a good replacement, I said to myself. I am young, active and companionable. And I liked grandma Lydia on first sight. She seemed dog friendly and keen on getting a dog, unlike the others who would come to visit the dogs and went, but were not interested in adopting any. Once, I almost cried when a little boy whom I really liked and who also seemed to like me took off after spending some time with me and never came back. A man who came with his wife spent a long time looking us up. They finally said they were going to think about adopting a dog for some more time. How fussy and indecisive people could be! Then another man took Roe, a husky but returned him to the shelter the next day. Roe was heartbroken.

When it was my turn for grandma to look over, I paraded myself around her prettily, wagging my tail vigorously, showing a few antics my buddies had taught me. I was desperately hoping she would choose me and take me out of the crowded and smelly enclosure I shared with a dozen dogs. More than anything, I longed to be in a home. One of my friends was in a home with an elderly woman who loved him so much. Unfortunately, the old woman got sick and died after having Leo for a year. Leo was devastated and would not want to eat for some time.

My heart sank when grandma Lydia left without taking me or anyone of us. "Did she not like me? But she spent more time with me than with the other dogs she saw. Another one of those uninterested humans who think that dogs do not have hearts! She was the fourth one who made me believe I finally found a home but rejected me. It was heartbreaking!

In the afternoon of the same day, I was taken out again to the meeting/ greeting room. I was sleepy and was disinterested to meet another human. I was surprised to see grandma Lydia sitting there with a female old dog, which she held on a leash. "Here you are! Lassie, meet…. What's her name again? "She turned to the worker who was holding me. "Tinsel." "Pretty, unusual name." She petted me lovingly, which seemed to suggest that she had decided to take me. No. I should not rush in my assumptions any more. I had had it too many times already.

"Mrs. Wade, let's give the two dogs time to get acquainted while we do the paperwork. "Paperwork? I never heard that word before." I said quietly. "You will like Tinsel, I'm sure,' the worker said. She is very friendly and would be a great companion for Lassie." "Bingo! I'm taken! I could not tell you how good that felt. I think I shed a tear of joy."

The car ride to grandma's house was short. We entered a two-bedroom bungalow, a corner property on a block at a senior community. I ran around the house enthusiastically, exploring every nook and corner. Lassie watched me happily too. She was probably lonely and found me delightful. We got along very well right away. I felt like I had found a mother. My real mother left me on a deserted street when I was just born. Good that the shelter people rescued me before I got hit by a mini bus. That was the saddest story of my life.

After romping around, I felt like going desperately. Where? I looked at the new, beige-carpeted floor with dread. But I had to go. Now! Pronto! Grandma was coming from the kitchen and caught me in the embarrassing situation. "Tinsel!" She half-screamed. I cowered in a corner expecting a kick in the butt. No kick came to my relief but I saw a look of dismay in her eyes. "That's it. She was going to take me back to the shelter. I resigned myself to the thought.

A day came and went but nothing happened. I felt lucky. Grandma would put us out in the yard from time to time, securing us with long leashes tied up to a short pole. A few days afterwards, a man came and put up a vinyl fence around the backyard. "Wow! It was good to run around outside without a restraining leash! I could now enjoy the breeze and the bird chirpings better. Most of all, I felt more free like I was out in the fields chasing butterflies.

One night a few months afterwards, as I was going to sleep in my comfortable dog bed, Lassie came and licked me repeatedly. She would go back to her spot near the bedroom door then would come back to me and licked me all over my body again and again. "What's the matter, pal? "She did not answer but I saw a strange, sad look in her half-opened eyes. The following morning, I was awaken by grandma's wailing. She was holding Lassie in her arms. Lassie was dead! I also wept. "So that was goodbye she was trying to say to me last night.

My misery did not last long. Bing, grandma's only daughter offered grandma one of her three dogs, Buddy. He was a stray dog, white, a male, Terrier/Sitzu mix thrown into the street by a heartless owner and picked up by Vanessa, Bing's friend. Her husband did not like dogs, so Vanessa gave him to my daughter. Buddy was not the friendliest of dogs, whose luck was like mine, a throw-away. He barked all the time. I did not like him at first, but we got along somehow because I needed a friend. I suppose he did too.

Buddy is a beautiful dog with white fur like snow and blue eyes. I could not understand why the previous owners did not like to keep him. He was a well-behaved dog, except for the barking. I observed that grandma liked him a lot, petted him more often than she did me. I would get zealous sometimes. I would edge closer to grandma to get her attention too, which she always did. I sense that Buddy likes me, goes around the house with me, even kisses me. I could not help but like him in return. We have become inseparable.

Summer Love

It was the middle of the day. The sun shone brightly and the heat was fierce. Alex was sweating so profusely he feared his perspiration would fall into the meats he was grilling. As he shuffled between the two grills, basting and turning over the chicken, hot dogs, and hamburgers, he cursed the intensity of the heat that beat on him mercilessly both from the grill and from the sun. The maple tree under which the grills were set up did not provide enough shade. The occasional breeze from the lake beyond the picnic area did not help either.

Josh, Alex' partner and in charge of the other griller had to leave suddenly because his wife was in labor at the County Hospital. There was no replacement. Everybody seemed to be enjoying himself/ herself, including half a dozen children and their grandparents, neighbors and guests of his sister and her family this July 4ᵗʰ weekend.

As Alex glanced at the big container of marinated chicken and meats, piles of hotdogs and hamburgers that still had to be grilled, he heaved a heavy sigh. "Torture!" He complained under his breath. He did not notice the young lady in a pink bikini approaching him.

"My hamburger is not cooked enough!" A harsh, loud voice made him turn around to face the lady who spoke to him like he was a hired hand. In his present discomfort, Alex had the mind to glare back at this impertinent girl he was seeing for the first time. Instead, he said as calmly as he could.

"Throw it back in, lady. Or would you like another one?" He selected a well done hamburger. The young lady ran off with her burger without thanking him. "Ungrateful, rude girl. A spoiled brat, I'm sure." He muttered to himself resentfully.

Alex had finally finished his chore. He had washed and changed his wet shirt, soiled apron and pants into a more presentable outfit and relaxed on one of the cushioned chairs in the veranda. "Alex, let me introduce you to one of our guests, Louella. Louella dear, meet my handsome brother, Alex." He rose, surprised at his sister's sudden appearance, a charming, dignified lady in tow.

Alex could not say a word for a second. He could only shake the lady's outstretched hand, stare at the smiling, beautiful face, and dreamy eyes who was staring at him with equal interest. Just then, another lady wearing a wrap around her bikini came up. She was a spitting image of Louella. "Oh, Cherry, this is my brother, Alex." Alex reluctantly shook the other lady's hand.

"Louella, tell mom I am going with Alon in his new Infiniti. I would be back home late." She disappeared without so much as a glance at Alex. "Sorry for my sister's behavior. She is the highly spirited one." Louella apologized for Cherry with a smile that charmed Alex completely.

"It's alright. You are most gracious and considerate. Care for a walk around the lake?" "Gladly." I need a walk too after two hours drive here from Naperville. As Alex took Louella's elbow, he forgot his misgivings of the day and felt he was more than compensated from Cherry's indifference. He even felt he just won a prize for the hard work he had put in that day.

He let out a long, happy sigh. Louella looked up at him inquiringly. Alex looked back at her, wanting to gather her in his arms and kiss her. He nearly did. Instead, he started to hum an appropriate song, "Summer Love." Louella joined him. The song became their theme song."

Moments of Triumph

I have had several "Aha" moments, times of triumph, jubilation and elation in my life. They were great, interesting and worth remembering. While a few remained in my memory for some time, two unforgettable moments stuck in my mind to this day.

After one year in Borno State, Nigeria working as an Education Officer, I was reassigned to the southwest of the country, to Abeokuta, Ogun State. I was to open the Home Economics Department at the newly founded Federal College of Education located in the heart of the city. To start a new department in an entirely new environment, in classrooms with the barest facilities, equipment, tools and teaching materials was very daunting and challenging. Needless to say, I worked very hard, often beyond work hours and even during weekends. I had only six initial students which grew steadily during the months that followed.

In the north, a similar situation confronted me but the expectations were lesser as it was a small, old Teacher Training College once managed by Missionaries in the 1900's situated in a tiny village deep in the jungle. In contrast, Abeokuta was a large city, the capital of Ogun State, with a school population ten times larger than my previous assignment. This new College was a Federal institution and the expectations were high. I doubled my efforts to live up to the expectations and beyond. My department grew from six students to one hundred and twenty students in two academic years, handled by four teaching staff including myself.

On my second contract a couple of years later, a team of evaluators from the Federal Ministry of Education in Lagos the capital, came to evaluate our college. They inspected the physical aspects of the new institution, facilities, supplies and equipment, records, staff qualifications and performance. The lady assigned to assess me and my department, a tough evaluator, remained in my department for one week. She went over my records, syllabus, files, outlines, lesson notes, bulletin board displays, teaching supervision comments, and students' projects.

She observed me during my lectures twice and my staff once each. She interviewed my staff as well as my students about me. She even followed me supervising Teaching Practice several miles off campus!

Three weeks after the thorough and tough evaluation process, I was called to a meeting of all heads of department. Report on the results of the evaluation covering some aspects of the college was read by the Vice-Provost. The results of the staff evaluation was read last by the Provost of the college himself.

I was completely surprised when he called me to the front of the meeting room and handed me a plaque. It said that I was the recipient of the coveted "Square Bracket Award," a national award for outstanding college performance. It was an award that was never before been given to an expatriate educator before. My co-heads of department applauded and congratulated me, led by the Provost.

My elation was heightened when I was interviewed by the local radio and television networks. When I appeared on the television screens, heard over the radio and featured in the local papers, I became an instant celebrity in the college. The NERC (Nigeria Educational Research Council) inducted me as a member. I was invited for speaking engagements at several Teacher Training Colleges in the country, was promoted to Senior Education Officer, then to Principal Education Officer.

That was followed by another "Aha moment" when I was selected as one of the outstanding contract officers working abroad a few years later in Manila. The OEDB (Overseas Employment Development Board), the agency that oversaw contract workers abroad had been monitoring our work performance from the start. There were only eight among hundreds of contract workers from different professions chosen to receive awards from the then, Pres. Ferdinand Marcos and his wife, Imelda, at Malacanang Palace in Manila in 1985. We received engraved plaques and cash awards of P15,000 (fifteen thousand pesos each. We were interviewed by television, radio and newspaper networks, appeared on television and on all the papers across the country. My relatives from all over the country sent me congratulatory cards, telegrams and letters. Those "Aha moments" gave me great personal satisfaction, a high sense of achievement and much happiness more so because they brought my family honor and pride.

Romancing the Snow

In my small town south of the Philippines, no one had either heard of the word "snow," or seen it. That was when nobody had yet traveled abroad. Sometimes there would be outdoor movies, showing cowboy films. They were real treats for everyone, especially for children like me. But we never saw snow in any of the films. Most of them were cowboy movies. They were mostly silent movies, black and white, shown by advertizers of prime commodities such as soaps and other household cleaning products.

When I graduated from high school and went to Manila to pursue my college degree, I rarely ever went to the movies, partly because I was deep in my studies and mostly because I had no money to spend for such a luxury just to see what snow was like. People who had seen it in the movies said it was like a miracle falling from heaven, all white like cotton. My curiosity was aroused but I could hardly even buy snacks with my meager weekly allowance. I only had enough to pay for my bus fares going to school and coming back. That was how life was for most of us. Nobody knew any better and nobody among my friends ever thought of snow.

When I went to work and live in another country, snow was unthinkable for everyone as it was warm throughout the year. And yet, sometimes, I wished I would see snow one day. I had read from magazines and newspapers how bad winter was in the U.S., in Europe and in many other western countries. I saw pictures of piles of snow almost covering the rooftops of low homes and streets, of people walking on the deep snow wearing long boots or children playing, building snowmen or skiing in the movies too. My curiosity of the white stuff increased through the media and through words of mouth. It had become almost an obsession.

My desire and longing to see the snow firsthand was finally realized when I visited my sister in-law in Ludwigsburg, near Stuttgart in West Germany. I saw patches and small mounds of the stuff while we were heading to my sister's home from Frankfurt airport. They were all around her front and backyard too. I gingerly picked some and held the delightful stuff, felt its soft, fragile nature. I wondered how different they looked from the movie filmed in Russia that I saw, wherein people were walking in knee deep snow and digging up the stuff from snow- covered cars. Skiers on the slopes of the Italian Alps in one movie all but fascinated me.

Was snow in Germany this scanty? I was shy to ask my sister in-law. When I was taken to the airport for my flight back, I saw snow starting to fall. They were tiny, white flakes that disappeared into the ground as they fell. Beautiful sight, but why did they vanish as they hit the earth? I became more intrigued than ever. But I kept my sentiments to myself.

Then years later, I came to live in the U.S. My first encounter with deep snow in New York was one of extreme surprise and wonderment! The stuff poured down incessantly for hours. When all was done, the snow measured at four feet! I ventured outside, walked on it, stumbled, then fell on it headlong. I exclaimed with glee as I scooped it with my hands, smelled it, even tasted it! I was like an innocent child seeing a toy for the first time. I longed to join the children in the neighborhood playing, hitting each other with the white stuff and sledding on the small hill behind our house. I joined them make a snowman but I soon quit as I was the only adult doing it with them. What an adventure!

Now? I could only look back at being naïve once with amusement. Ignorance is bliss, so they say but it could also be a humbling experience. I realized how innocent children feel, seeing or experiencing something entirely new to them, a joy that maybe fleeting but the memory lives in one's mind and sticks to the heart in its core.

Winter and snow in my older age are no longer amusing, as for everyone who is growing gray hair. Besides, too much too often could be tiresome. The honeymoon with snow is long over. Who wants the snow now and its accompanying discomfort, its ability to disrupt schedules, not to mention the depression it causes?

Still, wouldn't we all miss the cold and the snow when the weather is extremely warm? Or wish we would see the snowflakes again fall slowly like pieces of silver from the laden sky? Or maybe imagine yourself skiing on the Swiss or Italian Alps, or driving along snow-covered mountain slopes overlooking the frozen Lake Zurich? I would!

Oh, snow! Cruel, bitter sweet gift of nature!

When the Going Was Tough

I often tell stories about my childhood, of how happy I was with my loving and caring family, when the days were full of laughter, dance and music. The world around me seemed all beautiful and people looked free of care and want. Everything was as it was, until I grew older and got married.

On the seventh year of my marriage to a Marine Officer, when I was having my third child, clouds began to gather and slowly turned my world into gloom. My beloved husband, once the most thoughtful and loving spouse one could ever wish to have, changed. Was it his new position that changed him? Perhaps being captain on an ocean-going vessel demanded more of his time? When he was Third Mate, Second Mate then First Mate of the ship, he used to come home eagerly after two, three weeks or a month sailing the oceans. Now, the weeks turned into several months without him.

Time passed and he became more distant, his return painfully awaited and missed. His letters became scarce, then ceased completely. I was beside myself with anxiety. I was about find out what was happening, when one of his men on the ship somehow leaked his involvement with a woman in Singapore, his home port. To make matters worse, he cut off his allotment to his family completely. Left to pick up the broken pieces, I sought employment abroad with two purposes in mind, to provide for my young family and to try to heal a broken heart.

I worked my bones out, struggled to keep my sanity intact. Work and keeping busy are good antidotes to despair. Faith and hope are intangible and hard to reconcile, particularly for the downtrodden. But I never lost hope. Robert Gilfillan, a Scottish poet said rightly," There is hope for every woe, a balm for every pain"…My children gave me hope and prayers eased my pain.

However, there were times when I faltered and thought of ending my misery. When you love someone so deeply and that person turns away, the hurt is unfathomable. I contemplated driving deep into the jungles in Northeast, Nigeria, hoping that cannibals would eat me up, or drive into a deep cliff. I even toyed the idea of going to Singapore and kill myself in front of my unfaithful husband to make him sorry for himself. Horrible, crazy thoughts! Somehow, the better part of me nudged me back to sanity. My dear children, my angels, propped me up like strong pillars that kept me standing bravely upwards to face the stormy sky.

When the going was tough, I kept on going. And so, here I am, full of scars from my past battles for survival, weary but still alive and strong. Moreover, 'I don't allow regrets of the past embitter my present," a passage good to live by and practiced, written by Stansifer.

Call It a Miracle

One of my duties as Education Officer in a Federal College of Education in Nigeria, West Africa years ago was to observe Teaching Practice. This exercise was a requirement for N.C.E. (Nigeria Certificate in Education, a certification to qualify would be teachers to teach in the primary and Secondary Schools.

I had 15 hours a week supervisory duties in addition to classroom lectures, heading and management of the Home Economics Department. The students I supervised were from my own department as well as students from English/Yoruba, Music and Arts, Science Mathematics, History and Agriculture departments.

Our students, Year I, II and III were assigned to different schools in the city and in the suburbs. Some were assigned in schools outside the city and others as far as from 50 to 100 kilometers from the college campus. When I had to observe in far schools, I would stay in the Catering house or hotel for the duration of my supervision, depending on the number of students assigned to me.

On one particular day towards the end of the supervision period, I was driving along a long stretch of highway anxious to finish my supervision of two more students practicing in a secondary school close to the road. I was about to turn from the highway into a sprawling school compound when I found that my brakes were not working. No matter how hard I stepped, I felt like I was stepping into a hole without a bottom. I began to panic when my Volkswagen continued to run full speed ahead.

Ahead of me, there were two students walking close to the two-lane road going in the same direction as I was. There were other cars running on the opposite direction and behind me. To back out was not an option as I was on an incline. The road was also too narrow on either side to navigate away from the students. To continue where my car was taking me or to veer to the right edge of the road was a decision I had to make instantly. I opted for the latter.

Turning off the engine did not occur in my confused mind, only the lives of the two students. I felt my car leaving the road and flying into a cliff, like a plane about to land. It continued its flight past thick bushes and tall trees bordering the cliff. I closed my eyes tightly and prayed aloud." Lord! Save me!' I felt an abrupt jolt, and a loud crashing thump as if my car hit a solid object on landing. My forehead hit the roof of the car, my stomach pressed hard on the steering wheel and my knees felt like being squeezed by a hard metal.

I remained seated, immobile, paralyzed. I refused to open my eyes afraid of what I might see. "Was I a ghost? Are ghosts capable of thinking?" A rustle of something was coming down the slope. "Here! Here!" A man's loud voice penetrated through my semi-conscious mind. Another rustle joined the first one, then I heard feet sliding down and stopping where my car was. A loud banging on what was left of the driver' side shook me from my state of confusion. A strong hand touched my shoulder gently.

"Madam, Madam, Are you alright?' Was I alright' Or was I dead? My mind was still in limbo. "Oh, I guess so." I replied in a small voice uncertainly. The two men in white shirts and blue pants (college students' uniform) carried me out of the car and rested me on a log. "Rest here while I go get some help." The other student sat down beside me on the log, wiping away the blood from my cheeks and arms with his handkerchief.

Half dazed, I surveyed the wreck from where I sat. My car rested midway to the bottom of the cliff. It was kept from falling all the way down to the creek below by a huge tree trunk, like an arm supporting the middle of the vehicle and holding it firmly. The passenger's seat on the front was dislodged, the windshield was thrown off, the back seats were torn in half and the engine was thrown out of the car. Only the driver's seat, the steering wheel where my hand rested and part of the roof remained intact. My once sturdy little Volkswagen car was a total wreck almost beyond recognition.

I came out of the trauma pretty quickly and I recovered from my minor cuts and bruises within a few days. All my X-rays showed negative results. I only had elevated blood pressure, which was normal, the doctor said under the circumstances I had just been through.

That nerve-wracking experience was for me a lesson in Faith and Divine Intervention. Miracles still happen and they do happen when least expected.

Asian Trips to Remember
Tokyo, Japan

I had a most pleasant one week stay in Tokyo, the biggest city in Japan in 2011. The Japanese people whom I encountered were very courteous, always eager to please and accommodating. The only two things I had cause to complain about were that, many did not speak English, and that things were very expensive, from food to the least important items. The rate of currency exchange when I was there was 74.16 yen to a US dollar. The rate fluctuates every second or minute everywhere.

My tour included hotel stay, but meals were not included. Our tour guide was very friendly but sometimes struggled with her English with a heavy accent. On my second day, we visited the famed Tokyo Tower, higher than the Eiffel Tower in Paris, France. They are presently building a new landmark, higher than any such attraction in the world. Hundreds of tourists visit the tower every day. Even the six elevators could not accommodate all the eager passengers at a time. The top of the tower had unobstructed breathtaking view of all of Tokyo and beyond.

We stopped at a Buddhist Shrine of the famous Emperor Meiji and his Empress, and watched a royal wedding procession in front of the temple grounds. I had never seen such a colorful and unique wedding entourage before. My group and I watched the event with awe. The young, beautiful bride in traditional Japanese wedding ensemble was all covered with a white veil that flowed behind her. The groom was in his full regalia, with a sword (samurai) hanging from his left waist. All the guests in the procession wore colorful Japanese attires. They walked in small, quick steps. I forgot to bring my camera and so I missed taking souvenir pictures of the unique spectacle.

We visited the fort of ancient empires, surrounded by high stone walls. I wondered what were inside the fort. We did not have the chance to see the relics and mementos from World War II. We spent half the day the following morning at the impressive and attractive Imperial Palace grounds. Excursion inside the palace was not included in our itinerary. The Imperial Gardens were a sight to behold and to linger around in. Miniature trees and bonsai shrubs bordered the gardens.

After touring on my own around the gardens, I remained at the edge of the pond. To me, it was the most poetic and romantic spot in the entire gardens. A rounded pagoda- like structure on the side of the pond was a haven to sit and watch the white and gray swans as they glided around the pond, as if trying to provide entertainment to their spectators. The water in the pond was as clear as crystal, revealing the white pebbles that lined the pond's edges. Giant ferns, water lilies and flowers of myriad colors, an arched bamboo bridge and a promenade around the pond completed the magical sight. It was with reluctance that I left the spot to rejoin my group. We had a very delicious lunch at one of the restaurants located below ground level outside the Imperial Gardens.

Half of the day following was spent at the Ginza Shopping District. Our yen quickly diminished in the purchase of souvenirs which were irresistibly cheap. The Akasaka Guest House was an attractive western style palace built in Baroque architecture. We stopped at many other historic and cultural landmarks included in our itinerary. The last day of my stay was spent on a Sumida River cruise. The river ideally ran along many city attractions on both sides. Every side one would look were either historic or tourist havens, views of the old and new Tokyo. One would wonder how Japan recovered quickly from the ravages of World War II. Tokyo is one of the most interesting cities in Asia I had been to in my travels, so far.

Manila, to Misamis Occidental, Philippines

If you wish to travel to Manila or to any other big city in the Philippines, go in the months of October to mid January, to early May. Chances are that, it would not be too hot or too rainy as you would not feel the brunt of the Monsoon season. The southwest monsoon season that occurs in late May to December or January and the northwest monsoon season occurring in late January to early May could be very bad and uncomfortable, destructive and devastating. Very bad monsoon seasons had brought havoc, untold property damages, loss of lives, livelihood, etc. every year in this small island nation in Southeast Asia. Although there are areas that are not as severely affected as the others, most major cities in Luzon, Visayas and Mindanao, the three main regions in the country where most tourist visit, are almost always prone to natural disasters. The monsoon seasons bring with them floods, wind gusts as strong as 120 to 140 miles per hour or more, rains that would pour incessantly for days on end, as long as from seven to nine days, making everyone miserable.

With accent on the positive, let me reassure the traveler that we are not as expensive as other countries are, a boon to travelers. The currency rates go from P40 to P55 (pesos) to one US dollar. A hundred US dollars would go a long way in your shopping, entertainment and eating excursions. Our malls, which we have in abundance particularly in the big towns and cities could be compared to shopping malls elsewhere. Restaurants offer delicious selections of native and foreign fares at reasonable prices.

There are many tourist attractions all over the country that one could hop in, offering fine hotels, good food and entertainment. I could say with pride that the Philippines, termed the Pearl of the Orient is one interesting and worthwhile place to include in one's travel itinerary in Asia.

Filipinos are mostly Catholics, the religion handed to us by the Spaniards when they colonized us for 300 years. I think the percentage of Catholics is over 80%, the rest are Aglipayans, Jehovah's Witnesses, Protestants and other religious sects. Our prevalent religion is evident in our ways of celebrating special events, most particularly during Christmas, New Year, Easter and fiestas.(festivals) During these events, a special dish is always prepared in nearly every household, the roasted pig, or "lechon." Although there are variations in the manner of celebrations from region to region, most are celebrated in similar ways. We also have certain customs and traditions that we adhere to in spite of the advent of modernity and science advancement.

I have not been to my country for many years from the time I got married in 1975 and worked abroad to 2010, when I finally visited my home country. I felt a combination of sadness and of joy, particularly when I visited my hometown, Lopez Jaena, Misamis Occidental in the south of the Philippines. Things have changed considerably throughout my prolonged absence. I was amazed seeing the paved roads where once were but dirt roads or asphalt, the sprout of modern homes, restaurants, public places, electricity and running water and even internet! On the other hand, I was sad not recognizing most if not all the people I met, and in seeing our once proud farm and farm house reduced to a forest. I almost wept as I imagined my once upon a time childhood spent in that very place, now a far departure from what it had been. It was hard to imagine the neat, attractive home surrounded with all sorts of flowers and all kinds of fruit trees in the back and front of our house, mango, avocado, guyabano, guavas, and the vegetable patch planted with lettuce, tomatoes, kale, onions, etc. at the side of the house. The coconut trees that abound all around our farm house laden with fruit, the banana trees, jackfruit, and pineapples that filled the air with their delicious fragrance, were sadly all gone, replaced with thick bushes and wild trees. The area had become a forest. "One could not go home to his childhood again," one writer had aptly said. "But memories could make the past alive again," I hasten to add.

To go to my country from any port in the US is a long, tedious journey. If you go direct flight from Chicago to Manila, you would have only 4 to 5 hours stopover in S. Korea, Tokyo or Narita in Japan, then continue making your trip for 11 hours and a half total duration. Should you choose to break your trip, and remain in one of the stop over places, or reroute to other ports of call in Asia, is a matter of choice.

Puerto Princesa City, Palawan, Philippines

Puerto Princesa City, Palawan is located in the southwestern part of the country. If you look at the map of the country, Palawan is like a spear jotting out into the ocean, as if trying to separate itself from the mainland.

It is the home city of my deceased husband, Capt. Joel R. Amar.

Puerto Princesa is a bustling city, popular among tourists as it is the main port and is only a short 45 minutes plane ride from Manila or overnight trip by ship. It is bounded by oceans on both its narrow sides. The province has popular tourist destinations like El Nido, crocodile farm, Parks and recreation, picnic areas, first class hotels, white beaches and big market places that boast of all sorts of fresh and dried seafood, which you would not find in other places. The ocean surrounding the province provides ideal swimming, fishing, sailing and snorkeling opportunities. Offshore oil drilling also attracted many businesses to the city.

My mother in-law used to arrange a big picnic with the whole family to a beautiful picnic area, Balsahan, a good one hour jeepney ride from the city. Balsahan boasted of shallow, clear water, deep areas with diving boards, dressing and comfort rooms. Huts provide grilling equipment and tables for eating. Not so far away is the Palawan Penal Colony, where leprous people are housed. They are adept in doing all sorts of crafts, which they sell to picnickers in Balsahan.

I thoroughly enjoyed my sojourns in Puerto Princesa, the latest of which was in 2011. The place, like my own hometown is very dear to me not only because it was the place of my husband's birth, but because of my parents in-law, sisters and brothers in-law, who were loving and caring to me and to my children. Unfortunately, my parents in-law have already passed on, but I still have regular contacts with two of my sisters in-law, one now residing in Dublin, Ireland, and the other, in Herrenberg, West Germany.

Singapore, Malaysia

Singapore is one place in Asia that is haven to tourists all year long. A capital of Malaysia, it had been under the British until it was given back to the Chinese a few years back.

I had been to Singapore at least three times. It was my deceased husband's homeport. The port of Singapore is one of the busiest ports in Asia being accessible from the eastern, southern and western hemispheres. I would be happy to go back again and again to this clean, peaceful, vibrant and interesting city. It is beautiful by day with its high rise buildings that defy the sky and glittering at night with its neon lights lighting the city lasting through the early morning brilliance.

Shopping in Singapore malls and market places was a delight for me. You would find the finest "batik," a cloth material native of Malaysia and Indonesia, fine silk and a great assortment of ready-made clothing. My husband bought me dresses that fit me perfectly. Jewelry was fabulous and cheaper compared with other places. Most of my jewelry collection given by my husband were from Singapore. Watches, electronics and other modern devices and gadgets were remarkably fair priced.

Food? Oh, They are as delicious as one could imagine. They have very fine restaurants that offer out of this world dishes, local and intercontinental. I enjoyed very much each eating experience, whether at the hotel restaurants or at the outdoor open eating places. When we ate dinner at one popular restaurant, I had my first experience of eating seafood picked right out of the aquarium full of all kinds of seafood. It was a delightful and an amazing experience for me, one I often wanted to experience over and over again. I particularly delighted in sipping freshly squeezed cane juice from a long straw, bought at the sidewalk, while riding around in a tricycle driven by a local, wearing a very wide-brimmed- hat decorated with peacock feathers and a strange bright red outfit. I felt like a queen!

It would be nice to visit Singapore again to see the changes if any, since it was given back to the Chinese.

What Was It? (Fantasy)

"I am heading back home. Are you leaving with me, or would you want to stay longer?" Juan asked his friend Leo. "I am staying for a few minutes more. I hate to leave when the catch is good." Leo replied as he was putting bait on his hook. Juan rowed away with his aluminum pail full of squid, humming a happy tune as he went.

The two men were fishing two miles off the shores of their little town, this dark, calm night. It was squid fishing season. The men folk in town headed to the sea every night throughout the season and sold their catch the following morning at the town's open market. People from nearby towns came to their town mainly for squid. Leo and Juan, both fishermen since they were young, went out to sea as soon as it got dark. If they got back early enough, they would go from house to house peddling their squid while they were still freshly caught. This evening, they left earlier than usual and ventured farther out into the ocean to avoid competition from other avid fishermen.

Leo had three boys in high school. He hoped he would get a bigger catch tonight. School was reopening next week and his boys needed school supplies. He was whistling as he relished the thought of going home tonight with his pail and maybe the second pail full of fresh squid. His wife and children would be waiting for him and they would happily partake in a heavy midnight dinner. He kept on whistling to dispel the eerie and deafening stillness around him. He could not discern any of the other fishermen. He felt so alone in the midst of the expansive ocean.

His small kerosene lamp provided enough light to help him fix his bait and to see his immediate surroundings. He was about to reel in his next catch, when suddenly, he felt a strong hand grip his right hand holding the line. The grip was so tight and so sudden that Leo almost toppled over. Looking closely around, he could not see anyone, not even the hand that held him like iron. Overcame with fear, Leo froze for a second but he knew that he had to do something.

He struggled to free himself from the tight grip only to be wrestled off his boat. He fell into the water with the hand now holding his neck, pushing him down. Leo dove underwater, surfaced then dove again but the hand pursued him relentlessly. The "thing" seemed vent on drowning him. When the hand caught him again, Leo bit it with all his might. A blood curdling cry broke the tranquility of the ocean night air. The hand loosened its tight hold on Leo.

Leo saw an opportunity to swim away as fast as he could, leaving his boat behind. He finally reached the shore gasping for breath. As he collapsed on the sand, he saw his boat resting on the sand close to him. How did it get there? Did he not leave it behind in his frantic attempt to get away? And what was it that attacked him so fiercely?

A mystery.….

Thanksgiving

Thanksgiving! Gratitude! What worthy and pleasing words to say, hear and practice in our daily life. Thank you are words that give happy and satisfying feeling for the person they are said to and also to the one who give them.

I owe many people gratitude. I could not count the times I have said thanks to everyone, to anyone who had done me favors no matter how little they had been. Thanks or thank you are probably the most common and frequently expressions one says to a family member, to a friend or acquaintance, or even to a stranger. There are of course those who do not bother to say them maybe unintentionally, or out of lack of regard to the other person. Or they just do not want to be bothered. There are those who are born ungrateful and do not practice good manners and etiquette although these ideal forms of behavior can be developed.

Yet to express gratefulness when a situation calls for it does not cost anyone anything. So, having said that, I wish to thank my friends and relatives near and far who had been loyal, true and caring. It's been said that "thanks" is a small word but great to the sincere giver and to the appreciative receiver.

I would also wish to thank my immediate family who has given me the inspiration to carry on despite all the hardship, the problems and difficulties associated with day to day living. They have strengthened me both physically and emotionally throughout my trials and have given me the courage and hope when hope was almost nil.

But there is One Whom I really need to thank every single moment and day of my life, the Father Almighty. He had given me life, and that alone is more than enough to be grateful for. He had given me anything, everything that I am and I have, armed me with a strong armor to face the daunting battles of life. I would be nothing and would have nothing if not of Him.

My young life had been happy, but my later life was difficult and trying. I survived through all the hurdles, met the demands of my personal and professional life successfully, and had weathered the storms in my married life, unscathed. Now, I know not what are still in store for me out there, but I am certain of one thing, that He would never let me down. My hopes, prayers and trust in His mercy and love will carry me through and make the insurmountable become surmountable, as they always had. Such is my Faith, unwavering and strong. To sum it up, I have scribbled the following short prayer dedicated to Him, my Lord Creator and Savior:

"Thank You, dear Lord, My God!",

What would I be, Lord, if not of Thee!

Where would I be on this earth, full of sin and
troubles,

Weren't it of Thine Infinite mercy and boundless
love?

Who could I be amongst Thy creation great and
small?

From here thence would I go Lord? Be with me
here now,
Always and beyond!

I thank Thee Lord, I thank thee forever more...
Amen

Kindness

On my first day in school, a girl pinched me on the
arm and screamed, "That's my seat!" The teacher led me
to a seat away from the mean girl. She then confronted
the girl and said sternly. "Anita, you are being unkind.
Lydia is a new pupil. Be nice to her. That goes to all of
you, class. I shall reward kindness but rudeness will not
be tolerated." She took Anita to one corner of the room
and told her to remain standing there until recess time.
That was my first lesson in kindness.

At home one day, an old, poorly dressed woman came
to our door. She spoke to my mother incoherently. She
was stuttering so badly that it took my mother a long
time to understand what she was trying to say. My older
sister and I were laughing hard listening to the woman's

impaired speech. We even tried to imitate her. We got pinched on the arms when the woman had left with a bag of sweet potatoes and fruits that my mother gave her.

"How could you be laughing at that poor old woman? How would you feel if you were the ones laughed at? Be kind to people always especially to the poor and to the elderly. Kindness is the best you can do to others." These last words stuck in my mind. They changed my attitude from that day on.

Growing up in a large farm with my family of eight, we had hired farm hands to plant and harvest the crops. There were plenty of chances to be kind. I greeted the workers and helped serve them lunch. I also gave them water from time to time. I received a lot of praises, hugs and thanks. It made me feel grand seeing them pleased with me, even if I had to endure the dirt on my clothes and arms from their hugs.

As a teacher much later afterwards, I emphasized kindness in my classes in every opportunity I could. We held dialogues, pantomimes and games with kindness as theme.

Any act of kindness with classmates or with other school mates were rewarded with points redeemable in the form of pens, pencils, paper and notebooks.

An entirely different scenario manifested itself when I worked in a foreign country years later. I did not only experience rudeness, but threats to my very survival. Some people looked at me with curiosity, with derision and even with hostility. That was I think excusable. They must have felt scared or threatened seeing an entirely different human for the first time in their lives. Some of my college colleagues showed indifference too. I think they were envious of my success.

When I was petitioned by a wealthy family in Long Island, New York after the end of my contract in Nigeria ten years later, I was deeply hurt when I was treated like I had a contagious disease by co-passengers of a bus. Some preferred to stand to avoid sitting with me in the crowded bus.

I was hired by the Department for the Aging in New York a couple of years later as Case Manager and Entitlements/Benefits Specialist at Senior Centers in Queens. I did not feel welcomed during my first days at one center. One day, the elevator got stuck on the second floor of the four floors building with five seniors trapped inside. I did not know what to do! When they got out after 20 minutes inside the elevator, someone yelled at me. "What are you here for?" She gave me a cruel look. I felt like being slapped in the face.

Even to this day, some hints of indifference and unkindness still prevail. Have some people forgotten about kindness? It does not take an effort or cost any money to be kind and considerate of others, young, old, white, black, brown or yellow for that matter. A great writer once said. "You are at your best when you are kind to others." More beautifully praised by Addison," What sunshine are to flowers, smiles are to humanity. "I would like to add: "Kindness are like flowers to humanity. They brighten up one's day."

Con Artists

I had long planned to visit Egypt, the land of the ancient Pharaohs and pyramids. The plan was finally put into action in the summer of 2012, with two friends from New York, Thelma and Helen, during a 12-day Classic Mediterranean cruise on Norwegian Jade, a Norwegian Cruise Line ship. My cousin who had seen Egypt before told me that she was not impressed with what she saw during her trip there, that the two important cities commonly visited by tourists, Cairo and Alexandria were not the cleanest cities in the world. Further, she said that the only attraction in Cairo were the pyramids, and the Biblical Nile River in Alexandria. My curiosity was even more aroused. I had to see the places myself and form my own impressions.

Alexandria was the last port of call in our Cruise itinerary, originating from Barcelona, Spain to Athens, Greece, Izmir, Turkey, Valetta, Malta, Cairo and Alexandria, and ended up at Civitachia port in Rome. We remained in Egypt for two days, a day in Cairo to see the pyramids and a day in Alexandria to join a Nile River Cruise. It was hot and humid as our bus navigated through two lane dusty roads with piles of garbage on either side of the road and under bridges. It was apparent that they had sanitation problems.

While we were approaching Giza, Egypt where the pyramids are located, our excursion guide told us to be extra careful while touring and shopping at the pyramid site. Con Artists abound in the area. They had victimized a lot of tourists. You would be persuaded to ride on a camel and charge higher than normal rates. If you decide to ride on the animal, do not pay up front. If you do, the animal would go limp in just a short distance ride. Keep money out of sight because if they see you with a lot of cash, the vendors would bill you twice or thrice the normal price of the items. We were told to beware of their selling antics and of pickpockets, she emphasized.

I did not join my friends riding on a camel. I opted to just take a picture with the camel man riding on it. He charged me $5.00 for only one pose. I bought a hair clip and a native cloth handbag from a frail, old man and gave him a twenty dollar bill for $16.00 dollars, the price of the two items. While I waited for my change, the man demanded payment for the two articles. I vehemently argued with the man, telling him that I just handed him a twenty dollar bill and that he owed me some change. He screamed at me angrily. His former meek and weak demeanor turned angry and strong. I turned away exasperated as the other vendors, presumably his cohorts looked at me with malice. It was a no win proposition.

At the entrance to the Sphinx, a middle-aged lady was cursing loudly. She had just been conned of $50.00. She gave a vendor a $50.00 dollar bill for an area rug priced at $30.00. The vendor refused to give her the rug claiming that she had not paid for it. They screamed at each other for a while but she had to give up the fight. The other vendors menacingly surrounded her, scaring her off.

Sweating and exhausted from the hot midday sun and uncomfortable with my sand-filled sandals, I headed back to our bus, feeling I had not accomplished everything I had set out to see. I did not even go inside the pyramid. My interest in more sightseeing faded. I also felt disappointed in myself for having been conned. That was a first time for me. I realized I was not as smart as I thought I was. We had been warned after all!

Contemplating a come back? No thank you. The Nile River, which featured in the movie, "The Ten Commandments," looked unattractive and dismal with all sorts of garbage floating on its shallow and muddy banks. The unpleasant sights and disappointing experiences are more than enough to discourage an avid traveler like myself.

Childlessness

It took a year and a half after I was married before I conceived my first baby. My husband and I were looking forward to have a child earlier, but somehow, it eluded us for some time, resulting to so much anxiety for us both. His family and mine were large. I was the youngest in a family of eight, seven girls and one boy. Two of my sisters died during their infancy. My mother had the fewest number of children among her eleven other siblings. Each one of her brothers and sisters had no less than 10 to 14 children of their own.

My husband on the other hand had five sisters and five brothers, all living, he being the oldest son. There were two among his sisters who could not have children. One tried all efforts to bear children, medically as well as by quackery. All procedures failed. The other one adopted a three-month old baby boy.

Not having children in my country during my time was considered a cross or a misfortune. In those days, having large families was a status symbol. The larger the family, the more they were considered blessed and more well-off financially to be able to afford supporting their big families.

It was therefore with some apprehension that we looked at our future as an incomplete family. We began to question ourselves if one of us was infertile, or both of us? Someone advised us to see a specialist or take a vacation from work. My husband took off from his duties as a marine officer for a month. I conceived not long afterwards, to our great joy. It was for me a happy fulfillment of my longing for motherhood. My marriage took a more meaningful turn, even more so when our two sons arrived three years of each other's birth.

My sister in-law who tried hard but could not have children would often visit us and played with my children. I was filled with sympathy for her and her husband who spent hours with my children, take them to the park and to picnics. They liked my older boy so much, like he was their own child. They adopted two girls, but that did not help keep their marriage. It ended in divorce. The husband went back to Germany taking with him one of the adopted girls. My sister in-law did not marry again until many years later, to a divorced man who had children from the first wife. As with the first marriage, my sister in-law could not have children, but more reconciled with her being barren.

I had seen and heard about many stories of childless marriages ending in break ups, separation or divorce. Children are binding factors in husband-wife relationships. And if somehow the couple get separated or divorced in spite of their children, any one of the spouses who gets custody of the kids gets on with life just fine, with the children serving as inspiration and driving forces to carry on with life.

A child or children are blessings. Without them, a union is without its intended meaning- to propagate, to fulfill life's purposes. Marriage or union of two people without children is like a tree without fruit, therefore without value or importance.

Of Snow and Ice Storms

In the late spring of 1976, I set out to West Germany on my sister in-law's invitation. She was married to a German and was living in Ludwigsburg, near Stuttgart. Thinking that the weather would be milder during this time in that part of the country, I was not wearing heavy clothing. I regretted it the moment I stepped out of the plane and into the tarmac at the terminal. It was freezing cold!

There was no conveyor, so passengers struggled on the icy ground towards the arrival gate. The snow around Hamburg airport area had been cleared of ice but many spots in the departure and arrival sections still had ice patches on the ground. I was unmindful of the ice patches while I was anxious to see my sister in-law among the crowd of welcomers at the arrival gate. I slipped on the ice! I skidded and twirled about before I landed on my butt, skirt over my head, exposing a part of me. I was speechless with shame! A man held me up and escorted me into the building.

I thought the worst was over, but I was wrong. Not all the roads from the airport had been cleared. Passengers going westward were advised to stay in the airport hotel overnight. That evening, there was another storm forecast. As predicted, two more feet of snow fell on top of what was still on the ground. My sister in-law could not meet me until two days afterwards. Those ice and snow experiences were quite unpleasant, which I am not so enthusiastic to share.

The second experience was when I came to New York to take up employment in 1985 as nanny/governess with a wealthy Jewish family in Long Island, New York. My charges were a ten year old boy, and two girls, nine and six years old. They were cute children but precocious and naughty particularly the youngest one.

There was a big winter storm predicted to hit Long Island one weekend. People were apprehensive, recalling the devastating hurricane and snow in 1922 in the area. A calamity of that intensity could happen again this time, the weather forecaster said. We did all precautionary measures. We made sandwiches and stored them in coolers, baked cookies and other goodies. Shelves in the basement were stacked with canned, bottled and packaged foodstuff. Bottled water, flashlights and batteries, portable radios, even flares were made ready.

My hands were full with five young children, including two sleepovers. Keeping them busy was a task I did not bargain for. Each one of them wanted something different to do and asked for food all day long. The mansion became a madhouse with kids running around restlessly. Since the house cleaner could not come for her daily cleaning because of the impending storm, I helped the housekeeper tidy up the children's mess. The mansion had six bedrooms excluding the master's bedroom and the kids used all of the rooms, playing all sorts of games that came to mind.

The dreaded day came, but fortunately, only 20 miles per hour wind blew and only a foot of snow fell. After the yards had been cleared by the maintenance crew, the children begged to go skiing on the slope leading to the Olympic-size swimming pool at the end of the slope behind the house.

They skied for a while but someone thought of a different idea, to play jumping on the canvas-covered pool. There was no stopping them so I relented, much to my regret later on. The canvas gave way to their weight after vigorous jumping of as many as 10 small feet. All but one fell into the semi-watery pool. I panicked!

Inexperienced and scared, I did not know what to do at first, but seeing the children in real danger of drowning in the icy cold water, I jumped after them, winter gear on. There was not a moment to lose. Meanwhile, the one who did not fall ran to the house to get help. The children's father and a guest came running without coats on. By this time, I had managed to get two of the kids out of the pool. The other two were rescued by the men.

I expected a rebuke or worse, a pink slip, but neither came. The family was pretty kind and considerate. Maybe they were thinking that I was a neophyte in dealing with the snow, which truly I was.

Who Was He?

My friend Cecilia and I traveled a lot together. We had joined bus tours, land and air vacations and cruises when I was still in New York. In one of our package tours with

American Airlines Vacations, we went to Lourdes, France and to Fatima, Portugal. It was a one week vacation, with three days in Lourdes, France to visit the shrine of Our Lady of Lourdes and three days at the shrine of Our Lady of Fatima, Portugal. We went during the "off" season in August to avoid the huge crowds that would converge in these two popular pilgrimage destinations in the months of September and October. In Lourdes, we spent most of our time at the Grotto, where the Blessed Virgin first appeared to Bernadette, a young shepherd girl on October 10, 1858. On the third day of our stay in Lourdes, as we were leaving for the airport for our next destination, news of all land and transportation was announced. Not sure how we could proceed to Lisbon, Portugal, we wandered around the small town nestled at the foot of the Pyrenees mountain. We finally found a travel office and met a young man who could speak English. The other people we had asked help from did not speak English.

We were told to take a bus at the edge of the town that could take us one half of the long trip to the border of France and Spain. From that point, we could take another bus or cab to the border where we could catch our train to Lisbon, Portugal. It sounded confusing and farther than we had thought. But there seemed to be no other option for us. The long ride to the next station was tiresome and uncertain. We had to change buses at one station at some point.

With the help of a policeman, we got a taxicab who took us to the border of France and Spain, where we hoped a train would take us to the last leg of our journey to Fatima. It was now late in the afternoon and our cab bounced over rugged terrain, going through deserted, forested and bushy areas. I remembered my husband telling me about the Basque rebels that inhabited in the region. I became very nervous especially that it was growing dark and our cab showed no sign of stopping. We finally arrived at the train station at the border of France and Spain around 9:00 p.m. all shook up but relieved.

The relief soon turned into frustration. The trains at the station were also on strike! What to do in such a situation on a dark night at the middle of nowhere in a distant, foreign land was quite unnerving. I tried to speak to the four men huddled in one corner of the poorly lighted station, but none of them could speak English. I was like talking to statues. We were in that helpless, seemingly hopeless predicament when a man wearing a white shirt and pants suddenly appeared from the darkness outside.

"May I help you?' He spoke in perfect English without any accent. "Oh, yes, yes, Mister, we do need help... I stammered. "Follow me." He said briefly as he took our suitcases. We followed him unhesitatingly and without any questions to a trolley car that crossed a bridge spanning the river that divided France and Spain. As he was paying the conductor, I said, "Oh no, let me pay please." "I do this all the time Miss. Besides, you have no more francs. They do not accept dollars." How did he know I had run out of francs? I gave all our French money to the cab driver. And why would he do this all the time? I pondered on his words for a while.

We followed the man again through a dimly lit street without any idea where he was taking us. We were drawn to him like a magnet, unsure but confident. At the train station about fifteen minutes walk from where we got off the trolley, he pointed to a big white building all lit up. "That's your train station." He led us inside the building and deposited our suitcases near a bench.

"Please wait for me here, sir," I said to the kind man." To Cecilia I whispered. "I am going to pick up our train tickets. Make sure the man waits for me right here." I got our tickets and changed some dollars into francs to give tip to the kind gentleman. But he was no longer there when I got back. "Where's the man?" I asked Cecilia. "He was right here with me." We both looked around, but we did not see him. "That was strange." Cecilia spoke, shaking her head." Oh, he gave me this note." She handed a white piece of paper, but I could not read any of the words. The letters were all consonants.

Who was he? An angel sent by God to rescue two maidens in distress? This sweet thought prevails to this day and will certainly remain throughout all my days.

Embarrassments

Embarrassment No. 1

In 2011, during my planned trip to Manila, Philippines, I decided to reroute to Tokyo, Japan and remain in the city for one week to see its famed attractions. During our lunch on Japan Airlines, the last main meal out of three during the entire trip of 11 and a half hours, we were served an appealing, hearty lunch. There was one dish that looked entirely new to me. I have always been curious to taste new food, so I sampled the dish and enjoyed it too.

The aircraft was about to descend into Narita Airport an hour later, when I started to feel cramps in my belly. I ran into the washroom and let out everything I had inside. The flight attendant was banging loudly and repeatedly on the restroom door, asking me to return to my seat as the plane was about to land. I was sweating profusely but I felt much better. The curious look of my co-passengers made me feel very embarrassed. What were they thinking of me? A neophyte, ignorant first time traveler?

Embarrassment No. 2

In Tokyo, after a tour of the Imperial Gardens, the Pagoda Temples and the Tokyo Tower, we went into an underground restaurant for lunch. I sat with my group members at one of the long tables set for 12. The waiter took the orders of the rest, but he passed me. Later, he came back, asked my name and said that I was not on his list of diners. He asked me to move to another table at one corner, which was not reserved. I was feeling isolated and very embarrassed. The meal I paid for was delicious but I lost my appetite. How was I left out in the list by the tour guide and missed getting my lunch ticket?

Embarrassment No. 3

On my last day in Tokyo, we went on a Sumida River Cruise, then to the Meiji Temple, the shrine of the great Emperor Meiji and his Empress. I was so fascinated watching a colorful, traditional wedding procession of a royal entourage on the temple grounds. I got left behind by the rest of my group. They were now going to enter the temple but I was still far behind. I ran past the arched gate in order to catch up. A bulky man caught me and held me firmly by the arm. He looked very angry. He continued to hold me roughly, gesticulating and mumbling angry Japanese words, which of course I did not understand. I thought he was going to rob me, so I struggled to get away, screaming, but the man would not let go of me.

The man and I were engaged in a tug of war when another man, also a Japanese, came and said. "Lady, did you read the inscription at the gate entrance? This man is mad at you for disrespecting our custom." The bulky man finally released me. The other man led me back to the gate entrance. The inscription at the gate entrance said, "Deposit coins, wash hands and bow three times before you enter." I could not blame the man for being a patriot, but my embarrassment was great indeed!

The Psychology of Hope

Adversities, misfortunes happen all the time. Natural calamities, accidents, death in the family, serious physical or mental illness, incapacity, family break ups and other forms of problems are inevitable. They happen as surely as the rising and the receding of the tide, the rising or the setting of the sun.

Some unlucky happenings take place when one least expected them, resulting in more devastating effects to the affected. While some people have the fortitude to bear them bravely, nonchalantly, others take them seriously, affecting their behavior and outlooks, producing more complications, making things even worse.

I had rendezvous with misfortune several times in my life. As I look back, I only wish that I would never experience any of the same again, for I doubt if I would survive them anymore. However, who and what would prevent the inevitable to happen? Only death or mental incapacity could alter or stop one's predisposition to misfortune according to God's will.

But then, there is Hope. What is Hope? Is it merely a belief or feeling that someone or something will bring fulfillment and happiness, a strong tug inside that prods one to go on searching for a goal, or a reassurance that something one cherishes will be realized at last? Hope is beyond one's grasp at the moment, a longing, a wish, a look beyond what one's eyes could see, intangible yet gives solace or happy anticipation from a situation, which looks uncertain or bleak. It keeps one going forward with confidence, a conviction that something will turn out well or successful.

"I hope you will be well again," "Hope to see you soon," Hope you will still love me in spite of my infidelity," "Hope it will never happen again," "Keep your hopes high," etc. Hope is as many as there are situations and people who can think or feel, in effect, as long as one lives, he continues to hope. As long as there is life, there's hope," so the saying goes.

What about if someone says he/she has lost hope? Is there really such a scenario? For me, that is just an expression at the moment. I believe that a person who thinks or says he/she has no more hope is just desperate in that particular instant. Deep inside the person lies a feeling that is merely wounded or dormant for sometime but will wake up again at a given time. The situation may be likened to a cloud that blocks out today's sunshine and clears up again tomorrow or another time, as surely as the time comes and goes.

I continue to be hopeful. It is spiritually nourishing, a soothing balm to my pains and discomfort. It consoles me, brightens my days, strengthens my weakening resolve, prods me to go on and venture again into the world of uncertainty. I never give up and throw my hands in the air out of frustration. What difference does it make if the storm, hale, or the tornado comes, snow to fall or the earthquake to rumble and destroy? Neither you, me or any other could prevent them from occurring. There is one good thing that you and you alone could do for yourself, hope for the best.

My favorite writer, Bishop Fulton Sheen, wrote the following to describe Hope: "A person who has hope is like the boy who flies a kite. The kite may conceivably too high in the sky for him to see, but he can feel the tug of it on earth."

What a comforting, inspiring description of hope! Let us keep our hearts filled with hope in the midst of problems and adversities and look forward to happy days no matter what happens…

Town Fiesta

Town Fiesta or festival is a special kind of celebration that we had inherited from our Spanish forebears. It is celebrated in our town every year, on December 3 and 4 to commemorate the birthday of our Patron Saint, St. Francis Xavier.

It is opened with a Solemn High Mass in Latin and followed by a procession outside the church and around the block. Guests from neighboring towns would flock to our small town to partake of the elaborate celebrations. They would go from house and sample the special, local dishes and entrees. There is no need for invitations. Guests just come and go. Sometimes they say overnight or remain in a friend's home until the festivities are over.

The most common entrée was roasted pig, or lechon, a succulent, specially roasted pig stuffed with lemon grass, salt and other herbs. The roasting lasts for three to four hours depending on the size of the animal. Other entrees were pork adobo or asado, beef roast, sautéed vegetables, Fish Escabeche and other mouth-watering dishes. Households would prepare the entrees and desserts two or three days ahead of the event.

Desserts include a variety of native sweets. Commonly prepared are: Biko, sweet rice cooked with coconut milk and brown sugar, puto, steamed ground rice with sugar, baking powder, coconut juice and shredded coconut pulp and suman, also made of sweet rice, young coconut meat and sugar, steamed or boiled. The puto mixture is either steamed or baked in a native oven with coals on top and underneath. Leche Flan, a very delicious and more preferred dessert is custard made of egg yolks, condensed milk and flavoring which is either baked or steamed. Guests not only eat to their hearts' content but would also bring back home some food. The hosts would see that they do, a common Filipino act of extended hospitality.

The days' activities include parades, playground demonstrations, exhibitions, folk dancing contests and calisthenics participated by students from the local elementary school and high school. They compete with contingents from the neighboring barrios and town schools. Prior to the Fiesta Day, a queen, selected through money as well as beauty contest reigns throughout the event.

The town band provided all the music at the Mass and throughout the festivities. My father, a very good musician and music teacher used to lead the band. My only brother who could play the saxophone very well was among the band members. In the evenings, ballroom dancing, dancing contests and speeches by invited guests are held at the Municipal Hall. On the final night of the fiesta, movies shown by patrons from out of town and fireworks cap the grand celebrations.

Fiesta days in my small, remote town south of the country would forever be special for me. They hold lasting memories that I cling to through older age. I have seen and experienced all kinds of beautiful and memorable places and events in my travels throughout the world, but none of them hold lasting imprints in my mind as those I had experienced in my poor and humble town and its unforgettable fiestas.

Nostalgia overwhelms me whenever I recall those wonderful moments during my days of innocence in my place of birth, particularly during fiestas. It was a life devoid of care, loneliness, pain and anxiety. "Oh, that I could go back to those young days of bliss!

Opposite Poles Attract

Two women that I know are vastly different, not only in appearance but in their demeanor and character.

One is Lilia, a Filipino worker and the other is Funke, a Nigerian. Both are working in a Teacher Training College in one city in the southwest of the country.

Lilia is 40 years old, with brown and black complexion, with straight hair and brown eyes. She is petite, only five feet tall and weighs only 98 lbs. no heavier than a full, large size suitcase. She is soft spoken, eager to please and lady-like. She is deeply religious and never misses Sunday masses, is family-oriented and very conservative.

She has a Masters Degree in Education, teaches and heads the Practical Science Department in the college. She is separated from her husband and has three young children, ages 13, 9 and 6 years old, whom she brought with her to the African country after she was hired by the Nigerian Government as Contract Education Officer. She has two loves in her life, her children and travel.

Funke on the other hand was born in the south of Nigeria and is 54 years old. She is black, has short curly hair which she covers with a headdress, and has black, shrewd eyes, which are not too friendly. She stands at 5 ft. 7 inches, 180 lbs. and could lift Lilia without difficulty. She is married to a patient, persevering and complacent Nigerian husband, a successful businessman in town, who never leaves town and caters to his wife's every whim. She dominates him completely.

They have no children during their 25 years of marriage but do not want to adopt. Funke is a well known lawyer in town and teaches Political Science part time at the college. She is a tough, no nonsense criminal lawyer and had won 16 cases during her 18 years career. Funke is avoided and feared by her staff in the office, the criminals she goes after, and by her students. Once, she sent a male student to prison without a trial for screaming at her. She is loud, harsh, intimidating and fearless in court. Many times during litigations, defense witnesses are reduced to tears. She has received several threats during her dealings with drug lords and criminals, but Funke is undaunted.

On the other side of the coin, Lilia is well-loved by her students and respected by her colleagues not only because of her dedication and success in her profession, but because of her kindness and pleasant demeanor. She has a mild, well-modulated voice, could sing beautifully and could dance any of the modern dances gracefully. She has ideal social skills and has won plaques and citations for outstanding service in the college.

Funke never goes to church. She is not a member of any worthwhile organization that I know of. She met Lilia during a Department Celebration wherein she was among the important guests. She liked the Clothing and Arts Exhibits and bought a number of them. She commented highly on the items made out of throw-away materials. The recipes she tasted left a big impression on her so much that she asked for copies of the recipes. Lilia volunteered to give her a cooking demonstration of the desired entrees.

That was the beginning of a friendship that many did not expect to happen. The two are now often seen together in college functions, watching ball games together in the college auditorium and on the fields. Funke would invite Lilia to her celebrations at home or at her office. Lilia would offer to prepare dishes or snacks to serve to Funke's guests.

Though the two women are opposites in more ways than one, they get along very well together and become very good friends. Their relationship supports a proven science theory that, "Opposite poles attract, like poles repel."

Dust Gatherers

One of my duties as Case Manager and Entitlements/ Benefits Specialist at four senior centers in Queens, New York for eighteen years, was to visit the sick, the homebound, the bereaved seniors and to follow up those who were regular attendees in senior activities who had stopped coming to the center.

During many of those occasions, I would find the seniors' apartment or homes not only filthy but cluttered with all sorts of mementoes, gifts, souvenir items and objects. In some instances, I would send a cleaning woman to the home of those who were too frail to do cleaning paid for by agency funds. The cleaning lady would report back to me that the senior/seniors refused to allow her to touch any of his/her collections.

A sick senior whom I visited proudly showed me her "great collection" of native craft from her home country of origin in South America and stacks of other interesting objects from countries she had visited. The apartment looked like a craft store!

I shall never forget the day when I went to a 78 year old senior's house who was just bereaved. It was practically filled with all sorts of objects, which she bought from souvenir stores and garage sales, starting from the entrance to all the rooms of the house. She had spent quite a fortune for them, she told me proudly.

A male 80 year old senior who was about to move to an Assisted Living Program facility refused to leave behind his big collection of newspaper clippings dating back to post World War II period. There were old pictures of himself wearing a soldier's uniform and of others, picture frames hanging all over the walls, books, magazines, tea sets and china, which he said his deceased wife loved.

A homebound senior's refrigerator was so full of a quarter quarts of milk that when I opened the refrigerator, the cartons of milk, some already expired and had a rotting smell came tumbling out into the floor. The refrigerator door could not be closed tightly because there were many other kinds of foodstuff crammed inside it. It took me a lot of persuasion for her let go of some of the stuff. I told her that contamination from the spoiled food could cause illness. Her bed was almost hidden entirely with piles and piles of old and new newspapers and magazines. I had to beg her son who seldom visited her, to get rid of the fire hazards.

A couple living in a City-subsidized apartment had separate rooms and seemed to be vying in hoarding objects, some of which were rusting or rotting. Neither was willing to give up any of his/her collections. A shouting match ensued when the husband suggested to her to throw away some old, dirty pillows, blankets and some of her picture frames propped up all over her headboard. I asked the husband to just leave her be.

I would often marvel at this senior habit that appeared common among my clients. Were the reasons in order to cling to stuff that reminded them of their past, a leisure preoccupation or hobby, or a mere whim out of lack of things to do? Is hoarding a habit true to all those advancing in age? Or, God forbid, is it an illness or anything psychological?

The senior center's 82 years old secretary told me that she was going to empty her apartment of all stuff. She was sickly and would hate to give her daughter a hard time clearing up her apartment when she died. That was thoughtful and loving of her. Her apartment was amazingly clean but there was hardly space to walk around. Every inch was filled with figurines, stuff animals, wood carvings, fancy jewelry, different styles and sizes of lampshades and other pretty stuff she had collected over the years. Did I want to keep some for myself? She offered. I declined. I was not interested in collecting stuff then.

My 78 year old husband and I used to spend our weekends going to the movies, shops and restaurants, and yes, to garage sales too. He was interested in old paintings, workshop tools and old books, particularly history books. His room started to look like one of my clients' as well. He did not complain when I got rid of some of the stuff in his room and several tools in his basement workshop whenever he was not around.

When I retired, I found myself becoming fascinated with collecting stuff too, especially kitchen tools and gadgets, antiques and gift items. Soon, our basement was gradually filling up with things we did not even need. Did I catch the "dust gathering" fever?

When my husband died, I had to move to a senior retirement community close to my daughter's residence. I spent hours sorting out my "collections" to take with me. While we were packing things, my daughter said," Mommy, you are moving into a newly-built home.

Don't bring along your old furnishings and these "dust gatherers." They will only be eye sores and out of place in your new place of abode."

I have not given up acquiring stuff as of yet. Bargain hunting appeals to me and continues to be a preoccupation. What can I tell you? One thing good about it is, I give them away to agencies, like St. Vincent the Paul Society, The Salvation Army, or ship them to the needy folks in my home country. So, let me ask you, my fellow "dust gatherers," Is there a reason to stop my acquired habit?

Midnight Scream

My two close friends, Zenny and Luisa would occasionally sleep over in my house during weekend. Zenny lives with her daughter and her family in Elgin, and Luisa lives in Crystal Lake with her daughter and her husband.

They came one Saturday afternoon to spend two days with me. As it was Zenny's birthday the following day, we went to Mass at St. Mary's church and had lunch at Jameson's restaurant in Del Webb, Sun City. Zenny wanted us to try our luck at the slot machines at Grand Victoria Casino in Elgin and so that's where we spent most of the afternoon. None of us won any as usual. Last stop was at Spring Hill Mall in East Dundee. I browsed at Barnes and Noble while the two ladies went shopping.

On the two ladies' suggestion, I bought an Alfred Hitchcock DVD entitled "Psycho." It was an old horror movie but Zenny insisted to have a change from the movies we would usually watch, romance films. Last night, we watched love stories, "An Affair to Remember" starring Cary Grant and Deborrah Kerr, and "The Christmas Card" with John Newton and Alice Evans in the title roles. We had already seen these films many times before. Tonight, my two friends were anxious to watch a different type of story.

I hate horror movies, but I wanted to please my guests. Halfway through, I begged to be excused and retired to my bedroom as I could no longer stand the awful scenes. The two ladies continued to watch in silence. I could only hear the movie's faint, eerie music background as I prepared to sleep. Tinsel and Buddy, my dogs settled at the foot of my bed and were soon fast asleep.

A loud, frightful scream coming from the guest room where my friends were sleeping woke me up in the middle of the night. The two dogs barked and rushed ahead of me outside the room. "What's the matter?' I asked anxiously, knocking loudly on the guest room door, fearful that something horrible was happening inside. Luisa emerged from inside the room laughing. "Zenny just had a nightmare! It was the movie, I guess." "Oh dear, that scream was so loud and frightening! I exclaimed with relief.

"I am so sorry to cause you alarm. That Hitchcock film got into me. I should never have watched that horrible movie," Zenny said regretfully. "I shouldn't have either," said Luisa. Those terrible scenes are still vivid in my mind. I don't think I can go back to sleep. She picked up a book and went back to her side of the bed. Zenny went to the kitchen and came back with a glass of milk.

"Well, try to go back to sleep, girls. Tomorrow, we are going to the Triplex Cinema on Randall Rd. They are showing "Count Dracula and Son." "Oh, no, no! No more horror movie ever again please!" Zenny and Luisa declared vehemently. I turned around with a smile on my lips.

The Land I Love

I have always loved America. Since I was a child, the name, America has always been revered in my household consisting of my parents and six children. My parents always spoke of the country as our savior, our liberator from the Japanese, our most generous benefactor. The same sentiment was shared and nurtured by our countrymen. The feeling still prevails today, particularly among the older folk who had lived through the devastating World War II and the bleak period that followed it.

As U.S. goods: clothing, canned goods and medicines flooded our towns and provinces when the war was over, we could not be more grateful to our benefactor's generosity and benevolence. Countless American soldiers fighting side by side with our own men who joined the USAFFE (United States Armed Forces in the Far East) died in our country during that infamous war. What America had done for our struggling, poor country would forever live in the minds and hearts of the people of a grateful nation, the Philippine Islands.

When I was old enough to go to school after the Liberation, I continued to learn about America, whose most important legacy was Education. Every morning before classes began in our school, all pupils in the elementary and primary grades, their teachers and principal would gather in the school grounds, where the flagpole stood with the Filipino and American flags were hoisted side by side. Even the janitor (school maintenance man) was required to attend the flag ceremony every morning. We would sing the Filipino and American patriotic anthems and recite the pledges of allegiance.

During our music lessons, we were required to memorize and sing the American patriotic songs like, America the Beautiful, God Bless America, The American National Anthem along with our own patriotic songs. Our lessons in history always featured America. We celebrated our Independence Day on July 4th, the same day that the U.S. celebrates its Independence Day from Great Britain, until a few years ago when it was changed to June 12th, the day the U.S. gave us our independence.

We have as an independent nation learned to value everything American. U.S. made products were and still are considered of the highest quality. After the liberation, much of our culture and habits had been influenced by America: Our system of education, ways of living, our ideology, entertainment, modern technology, etc. Practically, everything available in America we also now have in the Philippines, particularly in the big cities and towns. We have learned to embrace everything American to the point of calling the attitude by some as "Colonial Mentality." Scores of Filipinos have migrated to the U.S. since the liberation and more continue to come in droves each year. In fact, Filipinos are among the highest number of immigrants in the U.S. now.

I have always dreamed of coming to this most powerful country in the world. I carried this wish since I was a child of 6 years old, when I had my first encounter with Americans.(soldiers) after the Liberation. Walking on the street in town with my older sister one afternoon, I saw a strange, peculiar contraption (army jeep) and men in green head gear (helmets) and greenish outfit (army uniform.) I was terrified seeing a thing with large eyes rolling on the street toward us. I tried to run away but the thing caught up with me.

One of the men got off, held me and spoke kindly in a strange language (English), which I did not understand. He gave me and my sister candy bars and chocolates. One of the men with decorated breast (medals) hugged me and held me up. The three men were very kind and even gave us more goodies. This first encounter with Americans have been included in my first memoir, "Grandma Series I."

Later on, I learned that they were American soldiers who came from a very far country across the continent to save us from the Japanese. My love for America and for Americans was born on that day. As I grew older, my dream to visit this renowned place became a serious quest. The dream became a reality many decades later.

A few years after the Liberation, my father had been asked by a close friend to go to Hawaii with him to work in a factory or farm. The salaries in dollars and benefits were attractive but my father refused to leave his family behind. My mother never stopped nagging him for turning away from that golden opportunity. She was more ambitious than my father, the kindest father one could ever wish to have. We would have been American citizens a long time ago if my father had listened to my mother.

Decades came and went. My secret wish was neither forgotten nor diminished. In fact, it became a passion or an obsession as the years advanced. When I heard of many Filipinos, some of them my friends who migrated and took up employment in the U.S., I was filled with sadness that I neither had the ability nor the means to realize my dream. I remained just a dreamer, like a love-struck admirer wishing upon a distant star.

When an opportunity opened up for me to go abroad, I wished I were bound for my dreamed country, my main goal. But it took more long, difficult years before I finally set foot in the land of promise, the land of my dreams. I felt I had been to a lengthy journey full of fears, trials and challenges then arrived at my coveted destination at long last. It was a grand, joyful feeling of accomplishment and self-satisfaction!

However, even a dream fulfilled and enjoyed could be marred with unwanted, and unpleasant episodes. I had experienced humiliating and disappointing instances when I first worked in New York. People I worked with and for, at a senior center treated me with indifference during the initial period. I believed the arrogance and indifference as merely being so because of the color of my skin.

I remembered my cousin, a USAFFE sergeant, who came to this country after World War II. He experienced an incident that made him vow never to come back. His wife and all his six children migrated to this country years later, but he could not be persuaded to follow them. He was a proud man who could not forget whatever experience it was that affected him badly. He later on revealed his resentment of the way he was treated.

I have also heard of many stories of discrimination among my friends who lived and worked in America. It was no consolation that immigrants from other countries other than the Philippines had had similar discriminatory experiences as well. I think some of the discriminating individuals have forgotten that they or their parents and ancestors were also immigrants once upon a time. Only the native Americans could be proud of their ancestry and could claim this land as their very own without question.

On the brighter side of things however, I can say without reservations that I could not be more proud to be called an American citizen. Having settled here firmly for thirty years, have known and met kind, considerate and pleasant American people, I consider America the best country in the whole wide world.

That is my honest perception after I have seen several countries around the globe. Regardless of isolated incidences of indifference and discrimination and challenging interpersonal relationships in this country occasionally, I would not wish to live any place else. My childhood dream started here and will end here, in the Land That I love. God Bless America! ! !

PART III

Dialogues (Original)

At Springhill Mall

Lynda and Susan met at the mall on a late Sunday morning.

Lynda: "Oh, Hi, Susan. What a surprise! I did not expect to see you here today. Where have you been all this time? I have not been seeing you in church for a while now."

Susan: "Oh, Hi, Lynda. I did not expect to see you today, either. You look fabulous!"

Lynda: Thanks for the compliment, dear, but I can not return your kind words, sorry. You look so much thinner than the last time I saw you. When was that?" She reflected for a second.

Susan: "I remember, at the Church Bake Sale last winter. Come, let us have lunch at the Food Court. I did not eat breakfast this morning."

Lynda: "No wonder you are so thin. Never skip breakfast, the most important meal of the day."

When the two ladies had settled down at a corner table, Susan remarked.

Susan: "So, how have you been and what have you been up to lately?"

Lynda; "I have had so much to do, attending meetings, gardening, food shopping and cooking for my daughter and her husband, and writing."

Susan:"How about travel?"

Lynda: "I have given up that hobby for two years now. The last time I went on a trip outside the country was in March, 2014, to the Bahamas with my oldest granddaughter. It was a present for her 16th birthday."

Susan: 'That was very nice. Tell me about your other hobby, writing. What are you writing now?"

Lynda: "Now, wait a minute. Is this conversation all about me?" She put down her fork with a piece of chicken and eyed her friend intently.

Susan: "Well, I'm afraid I do not have much to tell that you may like to hear." She suddenly looked sad.

Lynda: "Nevertheless, tell me. I promise I will give you a full account of the book I am writing right now. It is a romance novel, the type you like."

Susan: "O.K. Two months ago, Fred walked out on me. He said he was going to Honolulu to take up a job offer and will send for me when he has settled down. He never wrote or called. His cousin told me what he was up to. My good husband had left me for a nurse working at a hospital there." She wiped away her tears.

Lynda:" I am so sorry to hear that. That was cruel for Fred to do." She went around and hugged her tearful friend.

Susan: "I will be going home to Puerto Rico and stay with my daughter for a while. I might take up a job there if I can get one."

Lynda: "Listen, dear. Just call or e-mail me if you need anything. You have my number. Wait, how do you like to go to San Francisco with me? I am going to take the train to and from. I plan to go before the fall season. How about it?"

Susan: "No, thanks, Lynda. I have already packed. My apartment lease has now expired so I have to leave in three weeks. I shall keep in touch."

Lynda insisted to pay for their breakfast. It was the least she could do for a long time friend. As she had already bought the item she wanted, she offered to help Susan with her load of stuff. She shed a small tear as she watched Susan drive away home.

Halloween Blind Date

Scene: On the road, 5:00 p.m., Saturday, Halloween evening. Liza picked up her cell phone and dialed a number.

Liza: "Hello, Cecil! I am on my way to pick you up. Are you ready now?"

Cecil: "Sure, I am all ready. I am in my Halloween costume too. Are you?"

Liza: "I certainly am. Don't be scared when you see me."
 Smiling, while adjusting her witch hat.

At Drendel Ballroom, Del Webb, Sun City

Liza: Talking to a man wearing a cowboy hat and cowboy
 outfit. "Come, Carl, let me take you to your
 partner." She brought him to their table. "Carl,
 this is Cecilia. Isn't she gorgeous in her Cinderella
 gown?" Carl took Cecil's hand and kissed it.
Carl: "I am glad you have invited me. I am most honored
 to meet a beautiful princess tonight."
Cecil: "I am honored to meet you too. What kind of horse
 do you ride on?"
Carl: Takes his seat beside Cecil before his reply. "Oh,
 Misty, my horse died yesterday. I am a cowboy
 without a horse." They all laughed.

Liza left their table to mingle with some friends. The
two blind dates were engaged in intimate conversation.
They seemed to have forgotten that she existed. They
danced the night away oblivious of the merry crowd.

When Liza and Cecil were driving home after
midnight, Liza noticed that Cecil was unusually quiet.

Liza: "Pray, why so quiet, dear? Are you sleepy?' It took a
 while before Cecil replied.
Cecil: "I am far from sleepy, Liza. Tell me, how long have
 you known Carl?" She suddenly asked.

Liza "For five years now. He is a terribly nice man,
isn't he? He is a widower, for, let me see, I think for over

five years now, and ...lonely." She winked sideways to her friend. "Interested?"

Cecil: He has been very attentive to me during the ball. He did not even dance with another person throughout the whole time."

Liza: "I've noticed. He did not even dance with me. I felt jealous."

Cecil: To be very honest, Liz, I like him a lot. Thanks for arranging our meeting.

Liza: "I knew it! I think the feeling is mutual. When you went to the powder room, he told me he liked you a lot too, and wanted to know more about you."

Liza did not hear or see her friend for three weeks. Then, late one night, Cecil called her when she was about to sleep.

Cecil: "Sorry to call you this late, but don't faint! "Carl proposed to me this evening during our dinner date!" She sounded ecstatic.

Liza: "Just as I had hoped!"

Liza let out a long, contented sigh. Carl and Cecil were married the following year, with Liza as the bridesmaid.

A Strange Train Acquaintance

Setting: On the "Empire Builder Train, originating from Union Station, Chicago bound for San Francisco, California, month of September.

Scene 1: 5:00 p.m. Start of the two days, two and a half days journey.

Leonora: "Will you kindly give me an extra pillow, mister?"

Train steward: "Wait for a second, ma'am. An elderly woman two rows behind needs my help right now."

Co-passenger: Here's my pillow, Miss. I don't need it." The man seated next to her offered.

Leonora: "Thanks, sir, but this is a long journey. You might regret giving your pillow to me later on."

Co-passenger: Don't worry, Miss. I have upgraded my accommodation to a Sleeper."

Leonora: "So have I. Do you think we can get Sleepers soon? The conductor said all sleepers are full, and a few others have also requested upgrades."

Co-passenger: "Some passengers are getting off in Omaha, Nebraska. Here's your pillow."

Leonora. "You are so kind, sir. Thanks very much. I have a bad back. This pillow should help." An announcement: "A waiter is coming around to get your order for dinner."

Scene 11. 7:30I p.m. Dinner time.

Leonora: (She accidentally toppled a glass of ice water on the table for two.) "I'm so sorry. That was careless of me."

The man: "It's alright. It happens all the time. It won't drown me anyhow." He looked up at her and laughed.

Leonora; "Oh, It's you! A tiny world, isn't it?

The man: "It certainly is. No place to play hide and seek." He laughed again. Leonora joined him. By the way, my name is Armando, Armando Rosales. What's yours?"

Leonora: "I am pleased to know you, Mr. Rosales. Leonora Bermudez is my name. I am from Elgin, Illinois. Are you from San Francisco?"

Armando: "Very pleased to meet you too. I am from Manila, Philippines. Just visiting the U.S.

Leonora: Eyes lighting up. "You are from the Philippines? I am too, from the south. Been here in this great country for 29 year now. Not a Filipino anymore legally, but by birth, yes of course."

Armando: "Well, no matter where we are and what we become, we will always be Filipinos. Hope that does not make you sad."

Leonora: "Why should it make me sad? It's a fact. We never lose our identity even if someone erases our faces with a powerful eraser." Both laughed as they continued to eat dinner.

Scene III. Early morning. On the Train's Upper Deck

Armando: "Mind if I sit here with you? The scenery is breathtaking from up here."

Leonora, Surprised: "Mr. Rosales! Our world is not only small. It is cramped."

Armando: "Again, I would say, it is, certainly. Just as well because if it were big, I would not have seen you, or you me. It would have been sad. What are you reading, may I ask?"

Leonora: "Killing Jesus," by O'Reilly. Very moving and faith enhancing. It is a Best Seller. Wish I could be as good as he is."

Armando: "Are you a writer, then?"

Leonora. 'I am, an unknown one too. I have written four books, but I doubt if anyone would even look at their covers."

Armando: "You are too humble. I would enjoy reading your books, for sure. I am an avid reader of books particularly by female authors."

Leonora: Writing the titles of her books and handed it to Armando. "Look them up in the internet under my full name, or get them from the bookstores. By the way, why the preference for female authors?"

Armando: To me, women are very good in writing mild, interesting dramas, seldom about crime, violence and other undesirable types, with due respect to men authors.

Leonora: My books never fall under those you call "undesirable categories."

Armando: "I am sold. You are a very good salesperson. My first move when I get off is to search for a book store. I can't wait to get to my computer at home too."

Leonora: "I wish I had brought a copy of one of my handiwork. Anyway, I have given you my website and the name of the book store, Barnes and Noble."

Armando: "This trip is really fascinating." He changed the subject. "We are now passing through the second spooky tunnel. Yu won't be able to continue reading O'Reilly's book until after approximately 6 minutes. Did you notice that the Colorado river seems to follow us along the tracks like a slithering snake? I'll show you how enchanting the Colorado mountains are in the early morning glow tomorrow, as soon as the sun comes out from its deep slumber."

Leonora: "Why, Armando, you have a gift for words. She remembered someone just like him. "You could be a writer yourself." By the way, have they assigned you a sleeper yet?"

Armando: "Ah, yes. I got one last night, A Sleeper at the rear end. How about you?"

Leonora: "No, not yet. I won't probably get one at all. We have already covered more than half of our journey."

Scene IV. The Night Before
Arrival in San Francisco

Train Steward: "Miss, Sleeper No. 5 is now available. Would you like to take it? Someone gave it up for you."

Leonora: "Sure, I'll take it. It's time I rest my back on a bed. Which seat did this person move to? I owe this person, a thank you."

Steward: "He moved to the forward cabin, I think on Aisle 3, No. 13." Leonora gathered her belongings and moved to the Sleeper. She then went to the forward cabin.

Leonora: "Excuse me, ma'am. Where is the person seated next to you in No. 13?"

The old Lady: Nobody had ever occupied that seat since I boarded this train in Denver, Colorado. That was yesterday morning."

Leonora, bewildered. She asked a passing steward. "Mister, did you see the person who was supposed to be in this seat?"

Steward: No, ma'am. A man told me that he was sitting on that seat, but I never saw him there. That seat was never occupied since we left Union Station in Chicago. Perhaps nobody liked No. 13." He grinned as he walked away.

Leonora, to the Cabin Attendant: "Did you meet the person who occupied this Sleeper before me, Miss?"

Cabin Attendant: "Yes. Ma'am, an old woman. She moved to a Family Suite this morning with her granddaughter."

The first thing Leonora did when she arrived in her hotel in San Francisco was to check her e-mail. A message from her close friend in the Philippines startled her. "Your boyfriend of long ago, Antonio, died during a train accident between Manila and Baguio City three days ago. He was buried today. Pray for his soul."

Leonora: "Oh, my dear Antonio! Was that you then on the train? I did not recognize you. Thank you for the pillow, for the Sleeper and for your enjoyable company. Rest in peace now." Leonora wept.

Tragic Graduation Day

Scene I. At the High School Auditorium, Saturday, 4:00 P.M.

Marissa, to her husband, Cody: "I am very proud of our oldest daughter. She has been consistently on top of the class. We should not be spending too much in college because she has a scholarship grant."

Cody: "Indeed, dear. She is a Suma Cum Laude among the school's more than a thousand graduating students. Have you thought of a degree for her?"

Marissa: "I have suggested Law. We don't have any lawyer in the family. You neither. Everybody seems to favor the medical profession. We already have 28 nurses in my family and two doctors."

Cody: "My father was an Accountant, my brother an Architect and my sister, a Nurse Practitioner. My unmarried younger sister hinted Marine Biology as her choice."

Marissa: "We should not interfere with what our daughter wants as a profession. She had mentioned Engineering before, but she never brought it up again. Let us see what she decides. With her high school achievements, the sky is the limit for her to choose. The thing is, it must be her choice that should be respected."

The Marching Band started to play. The Emcee announced the start of the Graduation March, the first number in the program. The couple strained their necks in order to see everyone in the long line of graduating students. Someone in the crowd of guests made a loud whistle, and the stamping of many feet almost drowned the band music.

Cody: "How could they be so noisy? There is an important footnote in the Program to maintain silence throughout the ceremony."

Marissa: "Ssh! Here they come! Look how distinguished looking are the Principal and his Staff! Clarisse said she would be among the first batch, right behind the school administrators and staff, marching with the other Cum Laudes."

{The couple were very excited to see their daughter among the sea of proud candidates. When the names of the candidates were called one by one as they marched toward the center of the stadium to their assigned seats, Marissa and Cody could no longer hold their excitement. They joined the crowd's thunderous clapping and applause.

Marissa: "Look! There she is, with the blue cape and yellow band across her shoulders.! Do you see her?"

Cody: "Yes, I see her." (He focused his video camera on her daughter, while Marissa's digital camera was clicking nonstop.) The sound of clicking cameras prevailed in the auditorium air.

Marissa: Are we going to wait until the end of the ceremony? The speeches are boring me. Let us leave after this speech. I have to be in the front of the exit door to kiss my daughter and hand her our gift and this bouquet as soon as she comes out." She smelled the dozen red and white roses she bought earlier at the entrance of the building.

Cody: "Good idea! I have to take my daughter's picture as many as I could."

When the first batch of graduates exited the building, a big crowd converged around them.

Cody: "Oh dear, what a rowdy crowd! Do you see Clarisse yet?"

Marissa: "No, not yet, but I can't possibly miss her where I am. "Marissa was standing on a small platform just outside the exit door.

Cody, after twenty minutes scanning the faces of humanity around them: "Mari, what is keeping our daughter too long to come out?" Let me go back inside and check. Stay right here."

Cody soon came out and said: "Mari, I see no more people inside except a few school officials chatting."

Marissa and Cody remained long after the last crowd of people had gone, going in and out and around the auditorium, then to the office of the principal. No sign of the girl.

Cody: "Let's go home now, Mari. Who knows our daughter might have gone home thinking we could not wait for her?"

Marissa, wiping away her tears. "All right, but if she is not there, What shall we do?"

Cody: "Let's think about that when we get home. Meanwhile, I am very hungry and tired. You must be too."

At home. Midnight. The ringing of the phone woke Cody and Marissa up.

Cody. "Hello! Who is calling this time of night?"

Clarissa; "Papa, sorry for calling this late. I am at Miami International Airport!"

Cody: "What? Why are you at the airport? We have been looking for you! Are you all right?"

Clarisse: "I am alright, and very happy. Noel and I are waiting for our flight to Zurich, Switzerland, with an overnight stopover in Paris." (Giggling.) Marissa took the telephone receiver from Cody.

Marissa: "Clarisse, oh, my daughter! We have been crazy looking for you. Why are you doing this to us? Are you playing some kind of a joke?"

Clarisse: "No, mama. Please don't be upset. I just wanted to surprise you and papa. Oh, Flight No. 327, American Airlines is now boarding passengers. I shall call you again when we get to Paris. And, mama, papa, I am going to send for you when we get settled in Zurich. Noel"s aunt is renting a villa to us in Lake Zurich. Noel has a job offer there. Isn't that wonderful? I have to go. Bye!"

Cody: "Boy! Am I relieved that our girl is alright! I was going to report her missing tomorrow."

Marissa: "I am very relieved that she is safe after all, and happy for her. Let's go back to sleep now. We should hear from her again tomorrow, I hope."

Early the next morning:

Cody in a loud, voice: "Marissa, come here quick! Listen to the morning news!"

Marissa, rushing from the kitchen, was just on time to hear the rest of the awful news and see the wreckage of a plane on TV. "American Airlines Flight 327 from Miami International airport crashed last night halfway to its destination to Paris. No survivors have been reported".......She collapsed and did not hear the rest of the story.

On Board a Plane

Jennifer: "Excuse me, ma'am, but I have to go." Jennifer stood up from her window seat on Flight 18, Delta Airlines, smiling at the lady beside her.

Co-passenger in the aisle seat, Row 2. "Certainly! I will be going myself in a short while."

Jennifer: "Thank you, ma'am. I shall be at the rear, on one of the vacant seats reading a book." When Jennifer returned to her seat, the lady's eyes were closed. Jennifer remained standing, not wanting to wake the lady up.

Co-passenger: "Would you like to go back to your seat?" she suddenly asked Jennifer: "Oh, I thought you were asleep," Jennifer said, putting her seat belt on.

Co-passenger: "I don't normally sleep during a flight, no matter how long."

Jennifer: "That makes the two of us. I envy those who
sleep throughout the trip."

Co-passenger: "I do too. Are you a nervous passenger?"

Jennifer: "Oh, no. I am just uncomfortable with the cramp
position and the plane's movement, particularly
when there are air pockets. By the way, my name
is Jennifer Labore, a Publishing Consultant, from
Boston."

Co-passenger: "And I am Marian Campbell, from
Pennsylvania, a housewife and mother, anxious
to give myself a break from homemaking." She
extended her hand to Jennifer smiling.

Marian: "Pardon my asking. I have noticed that you
have been reading since we took off. Do you like
reading? What type of books do you like to read?"
Glancing at the book her seat mate was holding.

Jennifer: "My favorites are romance fictions and adventure
novels. Do you also like to read? "Jennifer had
noticed three books Marian put in the seat pocket
in front of her.

Marian: "I sure do. It is part of my DNA." She laughed
aloud.

The two remained quiet for some time until their
snacks have been served.

Jennifer: "Do you intend to remain long in L.A., Marian?"

Marian : "Only for a few days. What about you?"

Jennifer: "I have to meet some colleagues at our Publishing
Branch in the city of Angels. Maybe four days or
so, depending if I would find some surprises, who
knows?" She winked at Marian.

The flight attendant made an announcement. They were to land at L.A. Airport in thirty minutes. Both ladies continued their tete-a tat.

Marian: Where would you be staying in L.A., Jennifer? I'll be at Hilton, downtown. Maybe we could have dinner some time. At my hotel, yes?"

Jennifer: "That's great! I'd love that. I'm going to be at Hampton Inn. I'll find your hotel number when I get to my hotel.

Marian: "No need to do that. Here's my cell phone number." The two ladies exchanged cell numbers.

At the Luggage Claim area:

Marian, extending her hand to Jennifer. "Bye for now, Jennifer. I am very pleased meeting you!"

Jennifer: "Nice meeting you too. I'll see you again soon."

At the airport magazine stand, Jennifer picked a day's newspaper. It was her habit to know what's going on in the place she visits. As she was waiting for her cab, she glanced at the paper's front pages. An article at the middle of the front page surprised her. The familiar face of a woman stared at her. The caption said:

"A well-known novelist, Marian Campbell, is in town to promote her latest book, her tenth, entitled, "Spring Magic," a romance fiction. Signing of her books will take place at the Hilton Hotel lobby tomorrow, from 1:00 to 5:00 p.m."

The Stranger

Scene I. At St. Aloysius Church. Sunday, 10:00 a.m.

Norma and Thelma regularly go to Mass on Sunday at their small community church at the edge of town. They spoke in hush tones inside the church.

Thelma: "What are you going to do after mass, Norma?"

Norma: "To lunch at McDonald's on 47 Rd., then to Wallgreens to pick up a prescription. Would you like to join me?"

Thelma: I am going to Walmart to do food shopping, you know, my Sunday routine. I'd like to have lunch at the newly opened Denny's near the Mobil gas station. I have tried their Vegetable Omelet, and boy, did I enjoy it!"

Norma: I am inclined to go with you and try that Omelet, but I am not going to Walmart. My daughter did my food shopping for me yesterday."

The two women became silent when the priest's entrance hymn was sang by the church choir. After the First reading, Thelma nudged her friend.

Thelma: "Did you notice the man sitting at the right end of our pew?"

Norma: "No. (looking at the man.) I have never seen him before. Have you?" Thelma shook her head. During Holy Communion, the two curious ladies followed the man going and coming back from communion.

Norma: "I wonder who he is, and where he came from. We seldom see strangers in this small, sleepy town." Thelma and Norma proceeded to the entrance/

exit of the church after the mass. After greeting the pastor, they remained at the entrance.

Thelma: "I'd like to know this man better, just for the sake of curiosity. I'll wait for him right here."

Norma: "But I am hungry, dear. aren't you?"

Thelma: "Just a sec. Aren't you anxious to welcome a stranger? We don't see them everyday, you know." The two ladies waited but the man lingered inside the church.

Thelma: "I think we had better give up waiting for him. He might have gone through the side exit door. Besides, I don't want you to suffer from starvation." She giggled as she turned to go to the parking lot.

Norma: "Look, Look! He is coming now. Let me greet him first."

Norma to the stranger: "Hi! How are you? New in town?"

Gentleman: 'Oh! Hello! Yes, I am, just passing through your nice little town."

Norma: "This is Thelma, my best friend, and I am Norma." The man shook both the ladies' hands.

Thelma; "I am pleased to know you, sir,?"

Gentleman: "I am Lorenzo. The pleasure is mine." He bowed slightly. See you around, ladies. Enjoy this fine Spring day." The two ladies followed him with their gaze as he strode to the other side of the parking area.

The following Sunday, Thelma and Norma were surprised to see the man again, sitting at the same place as last Sunday.

Thelma: "Nor, I thought Lorenzo was just passing through our town? Why is he still here?"

Norma: "Maybe he had decided to stay for a while. Let's talk to him later after the mass." But they did not see him outside the church after the service.

The next Sunday, the ladies did not see Lorenzo at the mass.

Norma: "I guess our friend had gotten tired of our poor town. I can't say I blame him. For a young man like him and a good looking man too, a day is enough to see this whole, boring place. I even wonder why he stayed longer."

Thelma: "Well, there was something in that man, which interests me. I can't figure out what.'

Norma: "Oh, oh, don't you think you are past infatuation age?" She almost let a laugh. They became silent as the pastor started his homily.

Pastor: "My dear parishioners. I am very excited because now, we can put up improvements in our humble, old church. A generous man just gave us a big donation. I'm calling a meeting of the Church Improvements Committee this afternoon at 6:00 p.m.to discuss the project."

Thelma to Norma after the mass: "I have no doubt at all that our donor is Lorenzo. That's truly benevolent and generous of him."

Norma: "Indeed! I wish we had the chance to thank him." By the way, I am going to the Chapel of Our Lady of Perpetual Help. Coming?" Thelma followed her friend to the chapel. She lingered at the table where religious books and pamphlets were arranged.

Thelma, leafing through the Book of Saints, while waiting for Norma: "Oh, doesn't this man look like Lorenzo?" She said to herself, all shook up. She could not wait for her friend to come out of the Sanctuary. She whispered to her friend to come with her outside.

Thelma: Excitedly: "You won't believe this, my friend!" Look at this picture of St. Lorenzo! Isn't he the same man as our friend, Lorenzo?"

Norma: "Mary, Mother of Jesus!" Indeed, that's him! She crossed herself.

Thelma and Norma ran to the Parish Office to speak to Pastor Manny about their unbelievable story.

PART IV

Poetry (Original)

Poems of Love
I Remember You

I remember you-

When in the morning I awake, feel the gentle
breeze passing, caressing; when sleepy birds to
loving mates call to welcome the evening.
I remember your soft voice whisper sweetly
in my ears:" my darling! When in deep
slumber in my dream you appear.
When my face close to yours with tenderness
you lovingly kiss dear; when you hold
me tight and tell me I am dearly loved, I
remember with eagerness, with passion!
When you speak tender words of love, sweeter than
honey, I remember you, dear ! My whole life entwined
with yours, never ending devotion we once share.
When in winter you left me, happiness you
took, darkness obscure the morning sunshine,
banish the rays of ethereal glow!

I remember your solemn promise to come
back love, when spring comes again to cheer.
I remember the emptiness of summer though
the world around me is celebrating.
When autumn comes, the falling leaves
bring only sadness, despair; when all is still,
bleak, silence deafening, heartbreaking;
I remember you everyday throughout the dreary,
ever changing season; I remember you when it is
sunshine or rain, when I am smiling or weeping.
I remember you my love more than music,
poetry, laughter or tears; more than sweet
promises, priceless gifts and treasures untold.
When I am on the brink of passing, when
lights hang low, I shall remember you,
my beloved even more and more!

My Love, My Inspiration

Love, you are my inspiration! The core of my
thoughts, the ultimate of my desires! Beauty
may beguile, enchant, mesmerize,
The roving eyes may see, the loving heart may
not; I want your love, lest you forgot!
Inspiration! Truly you are, sweetheart! Roses bloom in
springtime, leaves aflame when autumn at its best;
Winter brings the darkness, melancholy prevails,
hurts; Flock of birds fly south seeking their next
nests, leaving their abode empty, filled with sadness.
Where's my inspiration, my true love? My inspiration
is gone forever; the barren, fields, once green and alive,
now dead; the snow comes with its bitter, painful sting.

My heart is empty, cold, waiting to be filled with
love, with inspiration, to survive. Let my world
brighten, rejoice and be glad when love is alive again.
Oh, where is my dearest love? Where thou hast
gone? Come back, my love, my inspiration!

Should I Forget?

I will not forget that you once loved me, lifted me
to the boundless skies, drowned with your kisses,
sweet caresses, sweeter than the purest honey.
I will not forget the loving words you spoke: "I love
you my darling, I always will!" uttered sincerely,
passionately, drowning me with pure ecstasy.
Your endearing smile haunted me, still haunts
me to this very day. The magic of your touch
always left my body on fire, my soul captive.
The memory of your love filled me with painful
longing when you went away; the glorious days we spent
together will live through eternity, Love of my life!
Is there a way to forget you?
Perhaps it is better to forget you and be happy again,
than to remember you, my beloved and be sad!

You and I

My heart leapt when I first saw you; you called my
name, your voice stirred my heart, lifted my soul!
We were together, you and I, no one else existed,
only you and I. The wondrous world glittering like a
thousand jewels when you kissed me, held my hand.

We strolled together hand in hand along
the streets, on the avenues aglow with neon
lights, all through the enchanting night.
The moon and stars flickered and lost their
radiance, as you held me close and kissed me, the
air filled with the music of a thousand violins!
Along the sandy shore we spent evenings
together, watching the flock of seagulls
flirting madly with the clouds rolling by;
The noisy bird chatter drowned the sound of gentle
waves lapping on our feet intertwined. All the world
stood still, the night air filled with soft laughter!
We climbed the grassy hill, lush, welcoming
valley its beauty enchanting, I adored. We
promised, pledged to be lovers always, born
to love and cherish through the years.
Our glorious, blessed true love, by Venus and
Adonis envied, infinitely lives beyond the
grave; Lovers forever more, You and I.

Poems About Nature

Is it Spring?

'All winter long I dream of springtime, Ah,
the agony of endless waiting! I'm lonely I'm
upset, the mounting snow so depressing.
I miss the song of birds, now their twitter
hushed; I long to see the green grass, the
flowers blooming in my garden;

Sad, long, dark nights, chilly air, not a
soul seen anywhere. Where is Spring?
Cheer me up! Banish the gloom!
Last night I heard flapping of many wings
across the clear sky; birds coming from
south to their nest at the park nearby?
From my back window, I see ships of clouds
rolling slowly by, like moving mountains, they
reveal the blue sky. Signs of Springtime?
When I woke up this morning, the snow is gone, blades
of grass, brown, dead or dying, struggle to greet the sun.
Patches of green beyond, refreshing green, some
lost from snow's heavy burden. Bare trees start to
awaken. I see a bird perched on a tree nearby, a
starling, a sparrow or a cardinal? Let it be Spring!
I hear clanging on Rte, 47, road construction
has begun in earnest! Lawn workers in the
neighborhood, tools in hand never rest.
In groups they toil, rake dry grass, gather dead
twigs, branches, sweep leaves. Sun's golden glow,
bright, glorious, a welcome touch on their skin.
Hurrah, I rejoice! Let the winter gear be put aside, the
windows open wide. For it must now be Spring at last!

The Magic of Flowers

Flowers in bloom! Flowers in bloom! They
warm my heart, they stir my soul.
Welcome spring, sunshine and rain, awaken
the plants from their long slumber.

Crocuses, tulips, Daisies, dahlias, zinnias,
roses, forget me nots, geraniums, intoxicating
hyacinths, multi-petals million flowers!
Delightful orchids, lilacs, daffodils, cosmos, violets
and a thousand more. Are they not wonders?
Their magic, enchantment fill the spirit with joy
and anticipation of glorious days ahead! Satisfy the
hunger for beauty, the longing for nature's best.
Tame the wild impulses, tone down the restless
mind, flowers are balms for the wounded heart!

Winter Reflections

The nights are long, cold, dark and dreary,
the days are short, sad, melancholy;
Where are the birds? I miss their twitter,
their loud, constant chatter,
Through my window I gaze at imaginary
stars, when will they shine again?
Unrelenting, unwelcome snow obliterate the
warm, beautiful earth, banish the green grass,
Blooming flowers I truly miss! Trees,
their leaves I long to touch;
I dread the roads, the highways covered with
snow, slippery, risky, I look at the skies, gray,
gloomy, foreboding, infinitely depressing;
I turn on the television, divert my attention, cheer up
my brooding soul! News are the same, more snow,
frigid temperatures, precautions advised, Keep inside.
What would a lonely, poor woman do,
isolated forlorn! Where's joy?

Winter is cruel, never pauses, unstoppable and
merciless to the weak; Yet it comes as sure as the
sun, persistent, unbounded, unhesitating.
It drags its feet, mimic the slow, taunts
the weary, desperate traveler.
I wish to see the moon, the stars to come again
through the blue skies! Their sparkling beauty
cast romantic spell to lovers everywhere.
To the lonely, they offer consolation, to eager
hearts, fulfillment, to the weak strength;
To the lost, a glimmer of hope, to the abandoned
sweet solace. Precious sunshine! Chase away
the gloom, banish desolation, welcome joy;
Winter, rain, snow come and go, when happy
spring comes, I'll rejoice with you!

Song of a Sailor

I come to you, sea of my dreams; Take me beyond
the horizon to glittering places on your shores;
Promise me fortunes untold, of priceless
gems your bosom holds.
For you I sing songs of gladness, of
sweet melodies I cherish.
I bid farewell to joys of childhood, I savor your
scent that enthralls, comforts a lonesome soul;
Your dancing waves smile, gentle
breezes the sailor you beguile,
Birds above flirt with your serene beauty,
in unison they sing with me.
Deep in you I sense a longing, a desire
to own, an obsession to prove-

Your power over me, your irresistible persuasion.
I sleep in your gentle sway, I dream
of your priceless bounty.
You are at your best when you are
calm, smooth, silent in prayer?
At your worst, threatening, when angry
fanned by the merciless wind.
I am tied to you, my friend or enemy?
Oh, unpredictable sea!
My life is now adrift, floating on your realm
like an endless melody. I came to you empty,
now I am full, should I continue to stay?

Dream

Who says a dream is just a dream?
Forgetting, unbelieving?
Some are mystified, ponder on it for long.
Talk about it, even write about it!
Others are happy recalling it, upset or cry over it.
Is it worth all the fuss, the confusion?
I say a dream may not just be a dream.
It has meaning no one can comprehend, explain.
It haunts, it bothers, it lingers or just fades way;
But It could come true one unexpected day!

Ode to the Ocean

You are the ocean, infinite, mysterious,
daunting, but welcoming!
You promise of adventure, hidden, great
treasures, untold, deep secrets;

Sea gulls fly above restlessly, endlessly
searching for food from thy bounty.
Rainbows over you, their myriad colors
enchant, touch you caressingly;
Life-giving breezes you fan, soothe,
comfort the desolate traveler,
Tiny, boats, great vessels you carry
on your shoulders gladly.
Amid the storm's onslaught you swing and you sway,
Your store of priceless bounty fills, satisfies the hungry.
You are the ocean, enigmatic, home to nymphs, sirens?
Mother earth holds you forever in loving arms firmly.
Life you maintain in mysterious
balance, never giving up!
Within your dark bosom man, sea
creatures, deities explore;
You need to be cared for, cherished,
immortal child of nature,
You are the ocean eternally powerful;
And I am just a man.

A Senior's Prayer

God, I ask of Thee countless things!
Would you mind, my Lord?
Good health, beauty and grace, success,
happiness, forgiveness and more!
Let me sing to you in thanks and praise,
your mercy infinite, relentless.
You comfort me in my sorrow, raise me up when
I stumble, give me hope when things go wrong;

You provide me with all I need and want, offer me
the best I should have, am I grateful enough?
Your smile is in the morning sunshine, in the
flower blooms, your voice in the whispering breeze,
your sweet, unconditional love fills every heart.
When I sleep you watch over me, when I
awake you prod me, make me feel strong to
face the uncertain, challenging day;
When I laugh, you laugh with me, and when I cry you
weep with me; each passing day You walk with me.
How great are you, my Lord, my Creator,
my Savior! Greater than the greatest, the best
of all the best the world could boast!
Yet I am feeble, prone to sin, sometimes doubtful
of your mighty power and mercy. Strengthen
my frailty, banish my infidelity, guide me away
from temptation and occasions of sin; Carry
me on your strong, mighty shoulders!
Most of all, forgive me, my Lord! Let me come
back to your welcoming embrace! Amen...

Poems About Patriotism

A Patriot's Cry

War! How cruel you are! devastating, ruthless, fearsome!
You plunder, you claim countless
lives, property and more!
You leave behind you, nations,
peoples in strife, desolation.
I loathe you, despise, deride and condemn you!
But you have no heart, no mind, evil is your name!

You took peoples' peace, happiness
and worst, their precious lives.
Though I fear you, I stand against your diabolic wrath.
I shall fight, defend my loved ones, my
countrymen, my beloved nation, to the end.
Although I falter, fall, I'll rise up again, Charge! I cry!
With more force, my strength my
body from agony, pain endures.
And if I perish in the battlefield, my soul will rejoice;
Stilll continue to fight till you are no more!

Prayer of a Soldier's Mother

Lord! My son is a soldier, out in a far, foreign land,
To fight the ruthless enemy, to
pursue the quest for peace.
Fight against nations captive in their
struggle for selfish goals;
His path is perilous, bloody and threatening,
Each day is uncertain, full of fearful
speculations: "Will I live,
Wounded or die? Will I see my loved family again?
Strengthen my faith in your saving power, dear Lord!
From the clutches of danger save my
son, my beloved, my life!
From gunfire, from treacherous terrain,
danger lurks everywhere.
Bring him back home to me, my
loving arms will comfort him;
Let me see his dearest, precious face again, dear Lord!
Let there be peace again! Amen.…

Arise!

Out of the clutches of fear, from the
agony of crippling disaster,
Arise, my beloved soldier, Look
up! See the victorious sun!
The conflict is over, rejoice, joy your
loved ones happily offer;
Thy comrades and thee we love,
we hail, heroes of the land!
Your strength, your precious life to
country you valiantly offered;
No greater love thou bestowed on homeland besieged.
The horrors of war, uncertain outcomes,
threatening clouds of defeat;
You confronted all challenges with
courage and with hope.
Now it's time to celebrate, don't look
back. Arise from your fall!
My dearest brother, my uncles, family
friends who served the past war,
To you all, your bravery we salute, we honor.
Your legacy of love, heroism, patriotism will live forever
In our hearts, in our lives through all the ages;
Arise now, fallen heroes loved forever!

PART V

Quotations, Sayings and Words of Wisdom, Written by Ancient, Renowned Authors and Philosophers

1. Doubt whom you will but never doubt yourself. Bonee
2. The virtue lies in the struggle, not in the prize. Milnes
3. Bad men excuse their faults, good men will leave them. Ben Johnson
4. Punishment is lame but it comes. Herbert
5. The falling drops at last will wear the stone. Lucretius
6. Every artist was first an amateur. Emerson
7. Study the past you would divine the future. Confucius
8. Good resolutions are a pleasant crop to sow. Malet
9. Men who have much to say use the fewest words. Shaw
10. The honor of a conquest is rated in the difficulty. Montaigne
11. In every human creation there is a chance of goodness. Seneca

12. Each morning, look upon your work of yesterday then try to beat it. Sheldon

13. Reason is immortal, all else is mortal. Pythagoras

14. When flatterers meet, the devil goes to dinner. De Foe

15. Fearless minds climb soonest unto crowns. Shakespeare.

16. Habit is either the best of servants or the worst of masters. Emmons

17. Be at war with your vices, at peace with your neighbors and let every New Year find you a better man. Franklin

18. To be proud of your learning is the greatest of ignorance. Taylor

19. A wise man thinks before he speaks, a fool speaks and then reflects. Delile

20. An honest man is the noblest work of God. Pope

21. Only the event will teach us in its hour. Shakespeare

22. People don't lack strength, they lack will. Hugo

23. The way to gain friends is to be one. Michelet

24. More things are wrought by prayers than this world ever dreams of. A. Christie

25. It requires greater virtues to support good than bad fortune. Rochefaucauld

26. They can because they believe they can. Virgil

27. It is not how much we have but how much we enjoy that makes happiness. Spurgeon

28. Man is not paid for having brains but for using it. Links

29. We hate some people because we don't know them, and we don't know them because we hate them. Colton

30. To be loved, be lovable. Quoted
31. No question is ever settled until it is settled right. Ella Wheeler
32. Twilight, the timid fawn went glimmering by, and night, the dark blue hunter followed fast. G. Russell
33. Beauty without grace is hook without bait. Emerson
34. The brief span of life forbids us to cherish a long hope. Horace
35. One may return to the place of his birth, but he can not go back to his youth. John Burroughs
36. Music is said to be the speech of angels. Thomas Carlyle
37. There is hope for every woe and a balm for every pain, but the first joys in our life never comes back again. Robert Gilfillan
38. No heart goes wrong that is told Goodbye, God bless you. Eugene Field
39. There never was a good war or a good peace. Benjamin Franklin
40. Oh, my son is my son until he gets him a wife, but my daughter is my daughter all her life. Dinah Craik
41. The reward of a thing well done is to have done it. Emerson
42. Every cradle asks, "whence" and every coffin, "Whither?" Robert Ingersoll
43. By the street of "by and by" one arrives at "never." Cervantes
44. It hurts too much to laugh but I am too old to cry. George McGovern

45. A good marriage is that in which each appoints the other, guardian of his solitude. Rainer Rilke
46. If we open a quarrel between the past and the present, we shall find out that we have lost the future. Winston Churchill
47. It is the dull man who is always sure and the sure man who is always dull. Mencken
48. The rain that makes things new, the earth that hides things old. John Mansfield
49. There are a thousand hackings at the branches of evil to one striking at the root. Henry Thoreau
50. Count where man's glory most begins and ends and say, my glory is I had such friends. Yeats
51. No matter what may happen, whatever may befall, I only know that I am mighty glad to be living. George Cohan
52. Mother is the name for God in the lips and hearts of small children. W. Thackery
53. The heart has eyes that the brain knows nothing of. Parkhurst
54. Ideas control the world. Garfield
55. A child is not a vessel to be filled but a lamp to be lighted. Author Unknown
56. Dignity is one thing that cannot be preserved in alcohol. The Christian Reader
57. What sunshine is to flowers, smiles are to humanity. They are but trifles to be sure, but scattered along life's highway, the good thing they do is inconceivable. Addison
58. Every child born into this world is a new thought of God, an ever fresh and radiant possibility. Kate D. Wiggin

59. The best way for a man to train a child in the way he should go is to travel that way himself. Author Unknown

60. The secret of getting somewhere in this world is getting started now. Hugh Allen

61. Love is to love the unlovable or it is no virtue at all, forgiving is to pardon the unforgivable, and to hope means hoping when things are hopeless, or it is no virtue at all. G.K. Chesterton

62. The five most important words are, "I am proud of you." The four most important words are, "What is your opinion? "The three most important words are," "If you please," The two most important words are, "Thank you." The least important word is "I." The proof Sheet

63. There is no surprise more than the surprise of being loved. It is God's hand on a man's shoulder. Charles Morgan

64. Blessed is the man who is too busy to worry in the day time and too sleepy to worry at night. Aikman

ABOUT THE AUTHOR

This is the sixth book written by the author. Her first was a family drama entitled Where Miracles Grow. The second and third are memoirs: Grandma Series I and Grandma Series II. The fourth is a romance fiction, Love Born on the High Seas, and the fifth is an epic romance novel entitled Love Born in the War Front.

She was born and grew up in the Philippines and has been living in the US since in 1985. She was a teacher for seventeen years in Manila, worked as an education officer in Nigeria for nine years, then was employed by the Department for the Aging as a Case Manager, Benefits/Entitlements Specialist, and Food and Nutrition Lecturer at four Senior Centers in Queens, New York, for eighteen years.

She has traveled extensively within the United States and to many countries around the world. Her book Grandma Series II: Grandma's Travels details her travel experiences. In between writing her books, she attends meetings with a writers' group at McHenry County College and hosts a radio show called The Homemaker with Lydia. This show is available at 101.5 FM, Huntley Community Radio, every Saturday at 2:00 p.m. and at HuntleyCommunityRadio.com.

Lydia Bongaron Wade